ESTH

MW01255130

HEALING FOR MOTHERS
AND DAUGHTERS

By Jodi LaRae Cunningham

Title: Estrangement: Healing for Mothers and Daughters

Copyright © Jodi LaRae Cunningham (2024)

Published by Authors on Mission

Contents:

Foreword

I'm a mom and daughter just like you. I have been fortunate to have time and resources to seek professional counsel from those with PHDs, doctorates, and masters since my estrangement began. Inside this book are the lessons learned and the disciplines I rely on to help reset my thinking for hope, love, and patience as I wait for estrangement to loosen its grip on myself and those I love.

Will you join me in considering estrangement as a mere phase in our intricate dance of life? For women who find themselves entangled in the seemingly conclusive step of estrangement, it is essential to perceive oneself as a skilled competitive ballroom dancer. Notice a dancer never stops dancing—even in place.

In the estrangement step, it is possible to keep moving. It is possible to move dynamically, balanced and securely, especially with a community that speaks hope into our lives. While we seemingly remain in place, may we be fully prepared to follow the next step into forgiveness, resolve, and resolution.

This beautiful dance between mother and daughter emanates a powerful sense of joy, hope, and love during moments of dynamic stillness. The music still resonates, so let us always remember that we possess the freedom to explore and express ourselves within the confines of our hold step: estrangement.

This book is full of biblical Scripture, but I wish to invite all mothers and all daughters to take what they can from these pages for healing within their own lives. All are welcome to join our community of women learning life anew within this estrangement step. As we look longingly for the restoration and resolve from the human fallacy that led us here, may we make our own dance beautiful by never stopping in our step.

We are beautifully and wonderfully made. (Psalm 129:14) Join us at Estrangement, Moms&Daughters on www.skool.com

Chapter 1

Healthy Expectations are Clear, Kind, and Known.

Expectations. We all have them, and when they fall short our emotions respond accordingly. Emotional pressure could be a signal that the health of our expectations may not be realistic. When we fail to consider our expectations, the chances of them failing others and ourselves is highly probable. This chapter will help us to discipline ourselves to be aware of the practice of clear, kind, and known expectations.

We all have expectations. So, why is it that we frequently overlook the importance of understanding our own? Forgetting to practice healthy expectations will challenge our feelings of security and leave us in the unknown.

Estrangement definitely has left us in the unknown but we can start learning how to cultivate healthy expectations right now, right here.

Take a step back introspectively. Take inventory of the skill of communicating healthy expectations as a practice. If we don't practice clear expectations internally, why should we be surprised when we have failed external expectations? We shouldn't. Personally, I desire to be prepared within my own expectations and communications. This is a lesson I practice, fail, succeed, and practice again.

In the past, I realized that my own expectations fell short for all, including myself. Perhaps I was lazy? Maybe I was overwhelmed? I definitely was unaware of the good practice of healthy, clear, and kind expectations.

I assumed my expectations were the same as others. I often knew what was expected of me—or so I thought. I was so unaware of my expectation practices being unclear; when I was disappointed, my exceptions were actually illusive to all.

I would wonder how I had become disappointed. Finally, when I learned the skill of asking myself what expectation was not met, I realized that my disappointment was a result of a misaligned expectation from every angle. All of a sudden, an unmet expectation of mine instantly became my fault, and no one else's. Or the unmet expectation was the responsibility of another.

Another possibility with expectations was often disproportionate external factors causing a lack of success or accountability to be clear, considerate, and fair. Expectations, like instructions in a recipe, must be known, understood and followed for a great result. For instance, a cake made without the proper recipe protocol may have to be served smashed, and in a bowl with a lot of whipping cream covering it up!

In example, take the average expectation of receiving a phone call. A woman waits all day for a phone call from her sister. The one who was supposed to call was unaware the other was waiting for a call that day. She had planned on calling her the next day, not that day. The following day, an uncomfortable conversation ensued as one sister had no clue why the other was upset about not receiving a call.

Each sister experienced a lack of clarity in timing concerning the anticipation of receiving a phone call. The confusion of the timing as to when the call back was coming created hard feelings. Each sister wanted to speak with the other, but the next day, neither even wanted to talk. Clarity is a good practice, but it is a practice.

As humans, we can experience expectations allegorically much like a ball in a game. If this metaphorical ball of expectations is dropped, lost, or someone simply decides to take their ball home, the game is over.

In my generation, we spent a lot of time playing in a nearby park. When a neighbor brought a ball to play kickball, we all had a grand time. When the neighbor who brought the ball experienced an unmet expectation, he/she would storm off with their ball. I can still hear the echo, "I'm taking my ball home! No one is playing!" There they went, leaving with their precious possession, the ball. That is a simple child-like example, but how do we act when our expectations are not met?

Before with your mom or daughter, you may have done everything together. Now, the divide has left you alone on the playground. Ask yourself, can you name the expectations your mother/daughter had? Can you name yours? Were either of you clear, kind, and willing to accept an unmet expectation from the other?

Are you willing to start to look at how unmet expectations definitely played a factor in "game over" inside of estrangement?

When I was initially assigned to a counselor after my children expressed their desire to have no involvement with me, I was completely distraught. I ended up being admitted to the hospital twice due to chest pain, and on both occasions, the doctors could only diagnose me with a broken heart. At that point, I simply refused to accept estrangement. I never expected estrangement, but I knew my children's expectations and mine had somehow ignited the schism.

I was in denial that we were in a lasting disunity breach. When I filled out a form with my new counselor, she said my children were estranged. I was not ready for her to say that. I said, "No, my kids are just mad and we will work this out. We always work things out." The counselor was right. I had entered into an estrangement. I never even knew I was in it. I never knew they had taken their ball of expectations and left the playground while I stood holding pieces of what was left of my shredded unkind, unknown, and unclear expectations.

That first counselor told me another very important rule of expectations that day. She said every success or failure my kids had after the age of 13 years of age, because I worked so hard to show them how to "fix" or "resolve" them, was not their win or loss, but mine. Wow! The independence I thought I was helping them gain was my dependency. Each failure and success had to do with me, not them.

In my efforts to help my children, they may have felt controlled. Children need to enter adulthood developing their own experiences of success or failure. After hearing the explanation of my folly, the counselor flatly stated, "But there are no guarantees. You can expect that." Sheesh! In my whole life as a mother, I never expected that the experiences I helped to create for my children could have an effect that would lead up to them wanting to do life not only independently, but without me.

The inability to fully comprehend the factors that influence our expectations can create a powerful barrier, leading us to feel disconnected in the end. Learning what we do not know, or experiencing moments we were never prepared for, are littered with blinding expectations of ourselves and others. To alleviate the sadness resulting from this lack of understanding, let's turn to a valuable lesson from Plato all the way back in 380 BCE.

Long ago, in Plato's *Allegory of the Cave* he demonstrated how misunderstandings are often a result of not having a fullness of sight or clear vision. It is truly remarkable that Plato's teachings continue to hold such relevance today. Plato's allegory helps us to be "others" focused, as we may not be as clear as we think we are, especially when expectations are involved.

Plato's (YouTube 2015) powerful attempt to demonstrate a lack of clarity to his audience, including modern women, demonstrates that the reality we perceive is often limited or possibly non-existent.

The Allegory of the Cave presents slaves who are chained facing the back wall of a cave. They cannot turn around, but instead must look only at the wall. Unable to see what is behind, they only see shadows on the cave wall in front of them.

Behind them sunlight and fire cast the shadows they see. The slaves mistakenly believe they understand what exists behind them. In reality, they have never seen the objects or individuals producing those shadows. This cave allegory sparked extensive debates throughout history within various realms such as government, academia, and society. Today, we can find the relevance of Plato's work especially in complex relationships like the mother-daughter relationship.

What can a mom actually see? What can a daughter actually see? As we reflect on the cave allegory, imagine the slaves being a mother and a daughter before their estrangement. They were chained in a cave, facing the back wall. From their limited perspective, they could only see the shadows that were cast on the wall they faced. These shadows create an illusion of reality for them, making them believe that they know exactly what is happening behind them. Remember, they only see shadows in front of them, not the reality behind. Of course the reader knows that these shadows are not an accurate representation of what is truly behind them.

One day, mom and daughter are freed from their chains and allowed to turn around and look outside the cave. To their surprise, they discover they each had experiences that were not clear or even a tiny bit true. They soon realize that a horse looks much more appealing and inviting to ride. The basket of apples does not resemble anything like what they had imagined while facing away from reality. The hump on someone's back turns out to be a woman carrying her child in a papoose. More and more, mom and daughter realize maybe each expected something that was never there—or at best was a partial reality.

Fortunately for us, we are not trapped in such ignorance within this metaphorical cave but we can use it to help us look more clearly at situations where we could not see plainly. Plato's allegory shows that our own perception may not even be true; at best, it is distorted. When it comes to relationships with mothers and daughters each can be blindsided by what is really going on perspectively, individually and as a collective whole.

Those trapped within Plato's allegorical cave were partially blind. Similarly, for us living with estrangement from our mothers, daughters or both, we experience cloudy vision. Could we be blinded from our own hurt from unhealthy and unmet expectations? Unlike the slaves in the cave, we have the ability to resolve for ourselves and to seek a clearer vision by dissecting and categorizing our own expectation practices or lack thereof.

Unmet expectations are like a chain keeping us enslaved because we may not see how healthy, kind, or clear the expectation was or is. It is important to remember that we cannot see others or ourselves clearly if we are living chained to the pain of an unmet expectation. When we actually dissect our unmet expectation, we may see it was quite unhealthy all along. Even if it was a good expectation, perhaps it was never clearly defined, known, or agreed upon. If we see an unmet expectation as unhealthy, it tends to lose its grip upon us.

It won't be easy to dissect all your old unmet expectations. I feel your pain, but remember, we can learn. We can wonder. We can take that first step out of this self-imposed cave of unmet expectations.

Keep one foot in front of another until each chain breaks away. Often we yearn for more, but consider this: When we realize that others can contribute to our fulfillment of expectations but are not the sole source of our met expectations, we can respond peacefully when expectations fall short. It is important to remember that accepting our daughter's or mother's lack of response or unmet expectation is an act of compassion.

Essentially, compassion is rooted in noticing expectations— all of them, not just the shattered ones. Write your fulfilled expectations in a list. These are the wins, especially if everyone benefited. Take the broken ones and put them away for good by acknowledging them and categorizing them. Take your expectations and ask yourself: Is this healthy? Known? Clear? Kind?

When examining our own expectations realistically and with compassion towards ourselves specifically, it becomes apparent how unclear they may have been for others and ourselves. When tackling broken expectations, start with the small ones first, leaving the big ones for last. This process will help you to build your practice and confidence from small achievements to the grander ones.

Have you ever paid off a debt? The key to success is to put your debts in order from smallest to largest. Then when you have paid off the smaller debt, take that payment from the smaller debt and use it to pay off the next debt. Soon you will have the payments free from the two debts to pay off the third. Then finally, the biggest debt you owe is finished. Each time a debt is paid off, the gains in hand to pay on the next debt will lead to a debt-free life. This is one way money managers like Dave Ramsey at Ramsay Solutions promote lasting freedom from debt. Likewise, by putting your broken expectations in order, you can clear them one at a time, the smallest to the largest. As you get stronger, you will increase your emotional intelligence to tackle the harder ones.

When reflecting on shattered expectations of the past, consider whether you effectively communicated them. Did the other person even perceive or acknowledge your expectation? Moreover, were you able to express it in a respectful manner? Was the other person even capable of fulfilling what needed to be done?

Moving forward, try evaluating your expectations before communicating them kindly with others. Practice having conversations about your expectations when alone, either by speaking aloud or journaling. Find a trusted friend who will keep confidence to practice with. The more you practice these expectation conversations, the more adept you may become at articulating your own expectations with others.

Visualizing and practicing conversation before you have them add value in building your compassion, clarity, and kindness—especially when you need to have a conversation you may not wish to have.

Here is an example: Mom and daughter have different expectations of talking on the phone.

"Mom, I understand that you want to have lengthy conversations, but I'm currently occupied with various tasks. I also miss you dearly, but my schedule is quite packed. Therefore, I can only allocate a 20-minute phone call on Sundays. Anything longer than that right now would be overwhelming for me given my busy life at the moment." In this response, you acknowledged your mom's desire for conversation and expressed your own longing to connect with her. Additionally, you clearly explained the reasons behind your limited availability for phone calls and provided a specific time frame that works for you.

Notice, redirect, and express healthy and kind expectations for effective communication. Practicing future conversations is a valuable drill. Find a quiet place and imagine the person you will have a conversation with in front of you. This can be your mother/ daughter/ or anyone. Here is a scenario of a mom/daughter conversation:

"I am your mother/daughter, and you are my mother/daughter. Expectations have led us down a dark path where we were bound to a wall, only catching fleeting glimpses of what could be or what once was. Mother/daughter, I am determined to acknowledge, redirect, express, and embrace healthy expectations for myself. Now,

I'm rebuilding my side of expectations where I wish to practice kindness and love. I want something new in which each of us provides a space for feelings of safety, appreciation, and affection. If, and when, you decide to return, I will take responsibility for recognizing my own expectations and how they might affect you."

Overcoming estrangement also involves dealing with unrealistic expectations. By freeing ourselves from these chains of unmet expectations through clarity in our acceptance of what truly is, instead of what we hoped for, helps. There is disparity inside of an unrealistic expectation.

For example, take a person willingly providing a service vs. a person demanding a service. The demanding person is often unrealistic even within the realm of customer relations in a business. Have you ever experienced the feeling that the expectations placed on you by your mother or daughter could be compared to the phrase "Dance like a monkey and fulfill my every request?" Notice, this could be very unrealistic and definitely not sustainable in business, or between a mother-and-daughter relationship.

As we step into the sunlight and out of our figurative caves, just like Plato's slaves did, we discover a whole new reality. We experience the warmth of the sunlight filling our eyes and touching our skin while we breathe deeply the fresh air. It is easy to breathe here. We bask in the light of truth. When, and if, our mothers/daughters find us here, we can have a clearer view of one another. In this radiant sunlight where nothing can hide—not even vampires—everything becomes visible and known. In these moments under the sun's embrace, let us see one another for who we truly are, rather than dwelling on unmet expectations of the past.

As time passes and we grow older, our vision becomes clearer as we do our own emotional relationship work. We feel free as we are no longer stuck in the past. We no longer react to unmet expectations so drastically. We now realize we could not see what was blocking our love for one another.

Allegorically, we are all living inside a cave because none of us were present at the beginning of creation. Job from the Old Testament was asked by God in *Job 38:4, Where were you when I laid the earth's foundation?* We may not know the reason for every detail that leads to estrangement, but by tidying up our expectations through clarity and letting go, we can find peace and calm within ourselves amidst even estrangement.

Unmet expectations are burdens too heavy to carry. Some are harder to drop than others, but some are simple to unhand. When we see an unreasonable expectation, that is a sure clue to release it. Rational expectations too are easy to let go of when the other party is incapable of fulfilling any part of a rational expectation.

I had a rational expectation in my late 20s when I was a volunteer Sunday school teacher in the four year old class. I spent almost two years running that classroom; I'd made a friendship with a woman whose two girls were in the class. Each was the same age as my daughter. I'd invited them over for multiple play dates throughout those two years.

We had built what I thought was a strong bond. Our girls enjoyed each other's company. One day, the church had a picnic. I needed to clean my classroom before heading to the

18

picnic. I asked the girl's mother if my daughter could ride with her to the park. I hoped she would be willing to keep an eye on my daughter and hers for 30 minutes before I got to the park. She flat out said, "No way, I'm not interested in babysitting." At hearing this, my heart felt the pang of an unmet rational expectation. I kept quiet as I heard her speak her truth as our daughters' hopes were dashed before each of us, as they wanted to go to the park together. She could have offered to help clean up the classroom with me so we could have all gone to the park together, but she did not. As I saw the sadness in my daughter's face, I thought "I'm glad she didn't take my daughter with her to the park; my daughter would have been on her own with no supervision."

In that situation, initially I noticed that my friend was unwilling to do a small reasonable favor for me, despite her eagerness for my free assistance in the past. However, upon reflection, I came to realize that she actually did me and my daughter a favor. My daughter remained safe with me, and it became clear that my friend was unable to provide any form of assistance in her own current circumstances.

I learned a valuable lesson that day about the power of perception of choice. Would the unmet expectation hinder or liberate me? We have the power to choose how we respond when our expectations fall flat. Our personal beliefs and desires may not always align with what others find clear or beneficial. A reasonable expectation may pose demands or burdens on others. Understanding this can help us to release the frustration of the experience of an expectation falling flat.

How many times, as mothers, have our daughters failed to recognize our support or assistance? In these moments did they understand the challenges we faced in our adult lives, be they with work, relationships with our partners or spouses, or even the pressures of caring for our own aging parents? As a mother, it is not easy to determine which information to share with our daughters. What should be kept private?

How often, as a daughter, did we express anger towards our mother because we couldn't stop the bullying at school? Or we experienced something distressing on the Internet that we didn't want to disclose? We all have external factors influencing us; each of these can impact the degree to which we fulfill each other's expectations. Striking a balance in communicating these complexities is rarely seamless. Forgiving in these moments can open a door to conversations when each is ready.

While going through a period of estrangement, it is important to cultivate healthy expectation reviews for yourself. Engaging in expectation management is akin to laying a sturdy brick as we construct a secure bridge for ourselves and others. Expectation practice serves as a solid foundation for rebuilding ourselves with resilience and affection, even when situations do not turn out as expected.

Are You Willing to Move Toward Clearer, Kinder, More Feasible Expectations? Let Go; Reset; Keep Going.

*Journal:

1. Recall moments when your expectations were not met.
2. How can you communicate expectations kindly?

3. What healthy, kind things can you do for yourself if your expectations are not met?
4. Identify situations in which unmet expectations have serious consequences.
5. Identify unmet situations for their clarity, kindness, and reasonability.

Chapter 2

Love and Grief

If we did not love, we would not know grief.

Consider thoughtfully the following recommendations while processing grief. These are suggestions from the International Fellowship of Chaplains.

1. Refrain from harming yourself.
2. Don't face it alone; seek support from others.
3. Expect that certain comments from others may trigger your grief.
4. Remember not to let the insensitive things people say leave you stuck in your grief.
5. Some individuals will bring your trauma or estrangement up without empathy or compassion. It's important to recognize that they are caught up in their own thoughts and emotions. Their fallacious thoughts are not yours. Keep their words out of your own mind space. Some might even use Bible verses to invalidate

your pain, but remember that their lack of understanding stems from not having experienced grief themselves yet.

6. Create a plan on how to respond to insensitive people assertively, with neutral tonality, and gentleness. I will say something like: "I'm sorry, but please excuse me," or "Please don't say that to me," or "I don't agree with you," or "Please be mindful of your words as they are hurtful unless you've gone through this journey yourself; it is difficult for you to know how I feel."

7. Most importantly, keep doing your own grief work so you will grow in your loss.

After my estrangement, I obtained my chaplain's license because I have encountered numerous individuals who've experienced grief throughout my life. I'm no stranger to grief myself. Throughout my adult life, I have resided in 15 states and two countries, allowing me to meet a diverse range of people who've entrusted their stories with me. These stories ranged from difficult to horrific experiences. Although I wanted to offer helpful responses and guidance for both myself and those around me who were grieving, I realized that I needed additional support to show them compassion.

Grief is traumatic. Grief does not go away, but we can grow through it and live a full life. We can also be very stuck. It's my hope that we keep growing in spite of love's companion: grief.

First, everyone experiences grief at some point—no one is immune to it. While we cannot prevent its occurrence, we can move through it with hope, grace, and self-care practices. Mothers and daughters will each face moments of grief throughout their lives; therefore, by learning how to grieve and heal within, we can serve as examples for one another on how to manage grief in a manner of quiet resolve and fondness for whatever or whoever we grieve for.

It may initially appear difficult to connect estrangement with grief, considering that our mothers and daughters are still physically present. It is essential to acknowledge that grief can arise from diverse sources, especially with estrangement.

Perhaps life's little griefs prepare us through practicing loss for the bigger grief that comes with the death of a loved one? This may be an unknown mystery to us now. Little pieces of our lives can show us how to understand grief, from the smallest loss to the grievous.

The loss of a pet, job, or enjoyed activity may all elicit the various stages of grief. Have you ever seen a person in denial or angry because their favorite sports team did not win? On Sunday afternoons during football season, sports fans get practice by grieving for the loss of a game. We may not agree that sport losses are a grief, but listen to these disgruntled sports fans closely. Grieving sports fans will say things like "You just don't get it; my team lost! That was not a real loss; it was the referee's fault! I'm going to BED! Just Leave me alone! I'm going for a run; I have to burn off this anxiety!" All of these statements fit into the category of grief stages.

Moving can also cause grief. I learned that relocating a child from one school or state to another could be traumatic and induce feelings of grief, especially if the move cannot be avoided. Through studying grief, I realized that my own children had experienced seven moves in their lives, and as a mom I failed to adequately process the moves as losses, which induced grief. Grief occurs when something or someone we love is taken away without our consent. In my family's case, my children felt the loss of leaving friends behind each time without their consent. The moves could not be avoided and each time the grief moved with us. In my case, a move for my children was comparable to a loss of friends, places, and things they cherished. Each was taken away by their parents' choices, not their own preferences.

Grief and love are intricately connected to the strength of our attachment. The attachment determines the intensity and duration of our grief. All we grieve, we love. So it is necessary to see the similarities between estrangement and grief.

As we progress through the stages of grieving, acceptance ultimately emerges as the final phase. Acceptance takes time and courage to wait upon. It feels known when one is capable of experiencing the pain of loss while still being able to function independently and finding joy in various aspects of life again. I can assure you that this is attainable because I am currently experiencing it myself after enduring various types of grief. You too possess the ability to reach this point. I promise. Keep reading.

Drawing parallels between our experiences and Mary the mother of Jesus allows us to see how even the most blessed woman in history faced grief (Keller, 2023). Mary's life provides valuable insights, especially for women. We can relate to her experiences as she was both a daughter and a mother.

Mary received grace and favor from the angel Gabriel as mentioned in Luke 1; they were given to her—not earned—

but given. Similarly, we became mothers without having earned our daughters; they were given to us naturally. Yes, science can explain the process of how babies are made. However, isn't it truly fascinating that women serve as the gateway for bringing forth our daughters?

It may be challenging to perceive Mary as someone relatable to us due to the distance of time and her son being Jesus, but try and imagine (Keller, 2023). Consider her surprise when she learned about her immaculate conception. Can you imagine explaining that?! In her time, this news could have led to severe consequences such as punishment or stoning by the community for being pregnant without a husband. Speaking with the angel Gabriel must have brought forth mixed emotions of excitement and grief due to potential negative reactions from others, including suspicions about the truthfulness of her story.

While we cannot know all the details surrounding Mary's experience, we can imagine that her parents worried about their daughter's situation. They may have been concerned about potential social consequences such as embarrassment or persecution if word got out about her pregnancy before marriage.

What of the grief of Mary's fiancé Joseph not wanting her after he heard she was pregnant? That was a grief or a loss—even if it was resolved. Joseph eventually married Mary after an angel assured him it would be okay in Matthew 1:20.

Later on, when Jesus was around two years old, both Joseph and Mary fled to Egypt together with Jesus to protect him from King Herod's order that all male toddlers should be killed

(Matthew 2:17). This event fulfilled what had been prophesied by Jeremiah regarding Rachel's lamentation for her lost children. The grief of this move—escaping in the night and knowing the little boys in the old neighborhood were no more—had to be a grief like no other.

Mary knew trauma and pain throughout various stages of Jesus' life. She constantly worried for his safety and witnessed his crucifixion years later. Is it plausible that some of the mothers who had lost their children during King Herod's order because of Jesus' birth, provided comfort to Mary during his crucifixion? These women would have understood the profound grief associated with their shared experiences over three decades previously.

By examining Mary's story, we can appreciate her mothering style and the emotions she likely experienced. Her grief must have been intertwined with joy making it bearable. While delving further into the theology surrounding Mary is beyond the scope of this discussion, it is essential to recognize that she also faced grief despite being hailed for her favor and grace as the mother of Jesus. Jesus, a son who performed miraculous acts had a mother who worried and grieved for him. I am not suggesting that our daughters are Jesus while we are Mary; rather, I want to emphasize how even someone in such a blessed position experienced grief in their life, too.

Through juxtaposing Mary's story with our own experiences of estrangement because of grief, we gain insight into how the most highly regarded woman—hailed with grace and favor— encountered grief throughout her life. Grief accompanies love on this Earthly plane; it feels inherently wrong compared to the essence of love itself. Yet through grieving and lamenting over our estrangements, we can gradually move towards acceptance while processing all the emotions these losses evoke.

Grief is an undeniable reality. It arrives uninvited! It hits us like a severe illness that requires time for recovery. However, unlike an illness that follows a clear path towards healing, such as resting and eating chicken soup for a fever, grieving operates on its own terms, without any specific timeline for resolution.

Life will never be exactly as it was before loss entered our lives due to estrangement or other forms of separation from loved ones. Life begins anew in grief. First we limp, then walk, and eventually run discovering new loves of many kinds. The caveat: we need to do our grief work.

The stages of grief:

1. Denial: Initially, it can feel unimaginable and unbelievable that such a loss has occurred. We may find ourselves thinking, "This can't be happening," or "Why me?"

The denial stage will be evident through one's responses. Many will refuse to accept the reality of the situations at hand. It will take time to accept what has occurred.

1. Anger: As denial gives way to acceptance, anger emerges fiercely. It serves as a form of protection for the love we hold within us for our mothers/daughters who have chosen estrangement over connection. We may catch ourselves thinking "How could she do this

after everything I've done?" or "This is what I get after all my sacrifices?" or "I'm so sick of her; I hate her."

This anger is profound and serves as proof that our love for our mom/daughter is still present. What? Really? Yes, let's check out when God was first angry and with whom.

God's anger is pure and good because it provides, protects and intercedes just as love does. Let us examine God's anger with Moses in Exodus. God's perfect anger provided, protected, and interceded for Moses and his people.

Exodus 3–4 points to how personal God was with Moses, even when Moses presented numerous excuses for not returning to Egypt to free the Hebrew people from Pharaoh's rule. Each time with God's perfect love guiding him, Moses angered God. For instance, God provided his brother, Aaron, as a mouthpiece to speak for Moses on his behalf as in Exodus 4:14. Again, in Exodus 14:15, God instructed Moses to ensure protection from the pursuing Egyptians by parting the sea for millions of Hebrews to cross through safely. Notice that in Exodus 14:15, God seems to question Moses' worries, suggesting firmly he should continue moving forward instead of fretting. In Exodus 15:18, God's anger is similar to pushing air out one's nose in frustration. Finally, in Exodus 32:7–14, inside of God's divine anger, Moses convinces God to show grace towards the ungrateful Hebrews. In each of these cases God's anger was written about because of human dread of no provision, no protection or no intercession.

We are not the God of Exodus(Keller,2015) (Gilbert, 2021), but Moses' account helps us understand that perfect anger is about protecting, providing, and interceding for someone or something we love. This thought can help us to reflect on the reasons behind our own anger. One effective method I found in dealing with my anger was asking myself questions like, "Why am I feeling so angry? What am I trying to protect? Who do I wish to provide for or intercede for?

This self-reflection brings forth anger as a prominent emotion during the grief process because we loved. Anger can stem from various sources such as the loss of time spent with a loved one, feelings of embarrassment, shame, or even pride. I have experienced these emotions too.

As long as we continue to love ourselves and cultivate compassion, we will gradually find that our anger subsides, showing us what and who we really love. Learning how to express anger in a healthy way by providing support and protection, as well as intervening when necessary, can become a powerful skill for humans—almost like having a superpower. Keep working towards acceptance even in the anger stage. You will get there.

1. Bargaining: In this stage, feelings arise where we try to negotiate with ourselves and perhaps even with our loved ones. We may believe that if we had done things differently, the estrangement could have been avoided. Bargaining involves thoughts like "If only I had..." or "What if I had...?"

Here is my best advice from my own counseling sessions during the bargaining stage: Refrain from making any major changes or purchases in your life until you have fully embraced the sense of estrangement. It is crucial to approach significant decisions with a clear and focused mind, driven by genuine intentions, not as a reaction to the pain within.

1. Depression: When bargaining no longer provides solace, depression sets in deeply and permeates every aspect of our being. This state of deep rest can make even simple tasks seem insurmountable. We may find ourselves sitting for hours without noticing the passage of time. Depression after denial, anger, and bargaining is the next step of grief because those three stages before, really wiped us out! Depression is normal when losing that in which you loved so much. Depression due to estrangement and all losses is "natural." [1]

2. Acceptance: The final stage arrives like a sunrise, illuminating our life as if we are the sole recipient of its rays. Though we still experience pain, our body begins to accept this new reality and adapt to it— recognizing that while holidays and special occasions may be missed due to estrangement, we have the power to make everyday moments meaningful, even in estrangement.

It's important to note that each stage may overlap and fluctuate. Their intensity over time as we work through our grief process will also fluctuate. Each stage becomes more manageable with practice, self-care and time. Reset, start over,

---

[1] Grief.com. " Because Love Never Dies." Accessed January 19, 2024. https://grief.com/the-five-stages-of-grief/

keep going, and count your blessings. We made it through another moment, hour, day, and chapter.

In conclusion, by engaging in grief work through understanding and experiencing these stages firsthand, we develop healthy ways of lamenting our losses while also recognizing our own personal growth along this painful journey that love has given us.

With regards to our personal journey through grief:

1. Utilize our gifts by sharing them with others.
2. Focus on building upon our strengths and nurturing our creativity.
3. Remind ourselves of who we are and who we are not.
4. Memorize this: grief is not a choice, but an outcome of love.
5. Understand that stress is part of being human, but we have the ability to respond from a place of peace.
6. Prioritize self-care, making it an integral part of our routine.
7. In moments of emergency or when seeking assistance, consider visiting the following websites:
8. https://grief.com
9. https://www.griefshare.org
10. https://www.thehotline.org
11. https://988lifeline.org

Chapter 3

Estrangement: What Are We Really Escaping?

Animals or prisoners in cages want to escape. Are we animals? Are we prisoners? No. We are mothers and daughters. Estrangement in the form of escapism does not resolve or reconcile.

Estrangement in the form of a separation may yield the ultimate goal of resolving and healing. Deciding to use this estrangement as a time of separation to explore healing and gain insight in order to resolve is loving—and especially kind to one's own self.

Some estrangement books I've read have chapters on how to escape one's own mind of the pain of estrangement. The chapters were focused on escaping trauma pain. However, the more I read, the more I realized that these books were pro-resolve of the symptoms and not the resolve of the root problem which caused the symptoms. These books gave me a feeling that one should keep estranging and escaping a family member instead of seeking to understand and to resolve for harmony, even if only with self.

Many social media posts would like us to believe we are justified in using estrangement as an escape and to punish another person. The comments on social media posts often reinforce cutting cruelty with the modern egotistical justification for executing estrangement escapism. The phrase, "death by 1,000 cuts," in the age of the Internet, should be "death by 1,000 comments." Estrangement escapism will often display itself as a bully on social media.

Estrangement, when used as a means to escape, is often proudly displayed as a medal of honor. It's worn as if granting power and control over someone else's confinement. Once, I confided in a woman I knew who had a history of estrangements about my work team's efforts to help another employee regain focus and resolve conflicts, but it proved to be quite a challenge. Shockingly, the lady I told in confidence urged me to never speak to my work teammate again. She vehemently expressed her judgment with harsh spitting words that sprayed across my face. I couldn't help but think my confidante was in more trouble than the woman my team was trying to assist in the meeting.

Governments that have separated from their neighbors do so to uphold war, be it cold or actively hostile. Isolating countries who chose to escape their neighboring countries, completely prohibit connections with them. With governments, wars have been the deciding factor to dig in and refuse the harming of the other. Cuba, North Korea, and even the Berlin Wall in Germany are evidence to this.

North Korea in its position of isolation hasn't solved its problems, nor has it made peace with their neighbors since 1948! What if North Korea actually ended their isolation which is now like a prison cell for those within? What if they tore down their barrier borders and learned to interface with the world like East and West Germany did with one another in 1989, marking the end of the Cold War?

What a joyous day when East and West Germany tore down the Berlin Wall in 1989! The dismantling of that wall served as a healing pivotal moment after World War II, allowing neighbors to once again see each other. That wall had been a reminder of one country who divided into two from what seemed like impossible odds. North Korea and Cuba are still isolated today, although Cuba is not as isolated as North Korea. The main point is that governments led by individuals who refuse peace and solutions for their people, cause their people to suffer from isolation where their problems are a constant reminder of resolution refusal.

Do isolated countries raise generations of people who are curious about the outside world? Do children from estranged families also wonder about unknown family members? Conflicts and problems are a part of life. We may think we can escape them, but can we really? Greek mythology did not think we could escape our fate.

The Greek mythology play written by Sophocles in 420–400 BCE titled Oedipus Rex was about the main character, Oedipus, trying to alter his destiny. It was foretold that baby Oedipus would grow up to kill his father, marry his mother and have incestuous children one day. Sophocles's play perhaps echoed the Greek thought and conversations of the day. Did Greeks believe fate was inescapable even if one tried? According to Sophocles, not even the lead in a story who was the son of a King could escape fate. Oedipus and his parents each met the fate they had dreaded. Each generation tried to avoid it. Throughout the story everyone knew of the prophecy curse and each did their part to keep it from happening. The attempts made to prevent Oedipus's future playing out so tragically actually caused the tragedy!

Did the Greeks in Sophocles' time know something about escapism, rarely solving anything? Sophocles wrote a story showing how trying to change a destiny only fulfills it. What would Sophocles say to us modern people considering the possibility of not facing our situations at hand—especially between a mother and a daughter? Perhaps he would say, "We may as well walk through it, as it will eventually be in front of us again." One can wonder.

I felt the sting of the ancient Greek popular thought after my 33-year-long marriage broke. When I was a child I had set a plan in motion for my own marital destiny. I was going to blaze the way for a thoughtfully planned future that I would be glad to be in. I carefully planned out my future and shared those plans with my husband. However, after 33 years of marriage, the very challenges that I had hoped to shield my family from ended up happening, in spite of my well-thought-out strategy. It was disheartening to witness the exact situations that I had wanted to handle differently or avoid all together, happen anyway. At that moment, it felt like my life was resembling Oedipus!

Estrangement as a form of escape has a penalty effect on generations. Often, years after an initial conflict from a divorce, adult children who finally meet up with estranged family members regretfully say, "I seriously feel deep sorrow for missing out on my auntie, my uncle or my cousins." I've personally witnessed estranged family members experience great value in resolution when they reunite with these once-estranged family members. What makes me pause is when the reconciled are bullied for not holding tight to the escaping estrangement practice. In this case, who's missing out: the escapee or the reconciled?

I do not support the idea of estrangement escapism because I fail to comprehend how avoiding a situation can seldom bring a resolution to a deep-seated problem. How does rejection help to understand the inner conflicts of the people who are trying to express their emotions through their pain?

However, creating clear separations until each party can heal may be in everyone's best interest. Instead of estrangement as a permanent escape, a separation time of estrangement may aid in the inner development for growth for everyone involved and future generations.

While we may succeed in distancing ourselves from others, we are unable to evade our own selves. It is beneficial to consider our estrangement as a form of separation, even if this consideration exists solely on our part. Within this separation, we can deliberately focus on our inner selves. We can utilize this period of detachment as a chance to confront our own selves.

As this chapter concludes, confronting four human traits that have the ability to hinder our personal mindset pertaining to estrangement are criticism, contempt, defensiveness, and stonewalling.

By acknowledging our own human tendencies to escape, consciously separating ourselves from criticism, contempt, defensiveness, and stonewalling helps to stay in communication with others. These traits often result in behaviors that ultimately destroy even the strongest of relationships. These relationship killers are referred to as "The Four Horsemen" by the Gottman Institute. Their name symbolizes their destructive nature; their name implies their equality to the Apocalypse in the book of Revelation. [2]

The four horsemen are relationship killers that absolutely fuel estrangement (List, 2024). Take the time to understand and identify when you are treating others with criticism,

---

[2] footnote Lisita, Ellie. Gottman.com. "The Four Horsemen: Criticism, Contempt, Defensiveness, and Stonewalling." Last date viewed January 19, 2024. https://grief.com/the-five-stages-of-grief//

contempt, defensiveness, and stonewalling. Then decide to stop these destructive behaviors within yourself. You alone control these horsemen.

The four horsemen will never bring any benefit to you or your mother/daughter relationship. They will only harm. Each will leave you feeling deprived, steal your happiness, and ultimately destroy everything. The most effective approach to defeat these formidable adversarial traits is to establish safeguards and refuse to engage in their destructive behaviors. Notice how stonewalling and estrangement act the same?

Stories of women who've managed to find acceptance and peace despite strained relationships with their mothers/daughters are a testament to this fact. Escaping may be a temptation in the moment, but stand firm. Show kindness and persevere through difficult times by seeking a separation as a time out to resolve.

Numerous women can relate to Joyce Meyer's stories on a personal level. Joyce had an incredible resolve to care for and help her parents even though her mom should have put her father in jail for his crimes against her. I personally know women who have experienced various forms of abuse during their childhood, and their mothers either turned a blind eye— or worse, blamed them for it. These women I met managed to find moments of resolution with themselves and eventually with their mothers. From what I have observed, all of these females had one thing in common: they took the time to sit with their turbulent emotions, sought healing and assistance, and finally stood firm in speaking truth to their mothers without resorting to confrontations reminiscent of the four horsemen. As they worked through their trauma, courage found them fully restored in spite of the past.

Reading this book on healing for estrangement shows we are trying to pursue a healthy separation for a period, rather than an everlasting estrangement. Often I will engage in a hypothetical game known as "now vs. then." Before our estrangement, the way each mother and daughter interacted led to the current situation. If you want something new later, then say to yourself, "Next year at this time, by learning to heal and love myself now, I will create a very beautiful life for myself, for others, and especially for my daughter/mother when she returns.

Women who are where they want to be now, did their own healing work to let their four horsemen go. For myself, my estrangement is only until my mother/daughter comes back. When they do come back, I'm working hard so that neither will find the four horsemen grazing in my pasture.

In conclusion, estrangement can be used as an escape route from painful relationships where healing has almost no chance, or it can be viewed as a separation time for all to take the opportunity to seek lasting healing. By facing our own emotions with a steady resolve, instead of running away from them or perpetuating negative patterns through escapism, we can work towards acceptance and freedom within these relationships.

The labor pains we endure throughout this process ultimately pave the way for a new beginning filled with peace and understanding even if the other side never restores. The side that seeks restoration through healing finds reconciliation with themself first; the side that uses the escape excuse only finds bondage of shackles where relatives are kept in a cage locked up with the key in their own hand.

Important: Estrangement can be caused by real physical abuse or threat. In these cases, please seek shelter. The National Domestic Violence hotline is 800-799-7233. National Eldercare for Abuse and Neglect is 800-798-7233. National Child Abuse Hotline is 800-422-4453.

Journal

1. Honestly spend time understanding criticism, contempt, defensiveness, and stonewalling.
2. Ask yourself, "Am I riding on one of the horsemen?"
3. If you are good at one of the horsemen traits, a certified counselor may tell you that was your coping mechanism as a child. Remind yourself you're an adult now and it is possible to self-soothe yourself positively to bring calm within.
4. When you return kindness to someone who is not kind, know you walked a painful journey well. You did your part in holding your calm. You can only do your side, not theirs. Resolve to do your side well, compassionately and kindly.
5. Praise, adore, applause, and complement; never criticize.
6. Approve, honor, love, respect, and reject contempt.
7. Aid, assist, help, and promote; drop defensiveness.
8. Honesty, understanding, communicating, inviting: no more stonewalling.

Chapter 4

Responding Within the Three Kingdoms

This chapter presents my personal thoughts and paraphrasing from the lectures with my professor, Dr. Shelley Hogan, at GCU in 2022. Categorizing situations into a kingdom type was the central theme throughout most lectures I had with Hogan. Keeping these kingdom ideas in mind, helped me especially work towards resolve.

Dr. Shelly Hogan has the visionary retreat center called E5 Life Strategies. You can find it at https://www.e5lifestrategies.com/about

A solid strategy for healing is understanding when we personally are not right with ourselves, out of step with others, and unfortunately when we agree with an enemy's influence. Knowing when we are dealing with the Kingdom of

Self, the Kingdom of Culture or the Kingdom of the Sinister (enemy), helps to organize our own thoughts and actions.

Understanding and organizing the moments of our lives within these kingdoms will give way for strategizing in order to resolve with self and others. Our estrangement arose from fear and confusion, but love is found in clarity and understanding. The Serenity Prayer is helpful when thinking of these kingdoms.

> *"God, grant me the serenity to accept the things I cannot change, the courage to change the things I can, and the wisdom to know the difference."*

The Serenity Prayer provides consistent and valuable guidance as we navigate through what is in our own ability to change and what is not. Millions deeply value this prayer due to its ability to assist individuals in finding the inward strength to bring about essential changes as they learn their place and actions within a kingdom. Moreover, the Serenity Prayer enlightens us on the importance of distinguishing between the power to modify or the willingness to accept what we cannot modify.

When we look through a kingdom periscope, we get a clearer glimpse of the way others see us, or the way we see others. Categorizing a strained moment into a kingdom shrinks it just enough to find a healthy resolve in its rightful kingdom.

The easiest kingdom for me, is the Kingdom of the Sinister— or the enemy. I like the word "sinister" over the enemy because the smallest white lie to the most grievous manipulations is sinister. Can't we all see the smirk on a character like Nellie Olsen from the Little House on the Prairie toward Laura Ingles? Wow, does that trigger me to want to foil Nellie Olson's sinister plots. We can also see someone controlled by the monsters of WW1 and WW2 in a sinister fashion. Somewhere in the middle, each one of the enemy plots are found. As we pinpoint a human behavior as agreeing with an enemy, or manipulating to deflect and blame others, we have successfully labeled that act as Kingdom of the Sinister weaponry.

Often the enemy kingdom in western cultures isn't considered first. All across the continent of Africa, the sinister is widely recognized and often the initial focus when seeking a solution to end an infraction. Some people live in fear or dread about the enemy's camp. The good news is that we can and do have authority to categorize this sinister camp and put it in its place, far from our reach! We can speak against it; we can pray against it and we can speak a Bible verse towards it. Don't forget, the Kingdom of the Sinister may influence the personal and the cultural, but it does not have to if we are alert and guard our own inner thoughts and actions.

Experiencing confusion can be a clear sign that the sinister camp is at work. When there is confusion, the disruption of the beauty meant for self and others could have an ominous influence. The behavior undercover may be pride, gossip, lies, impatience, accusations, condemnation, etc. If we are not alert, we may be tempted to agree with each of these thoughts. When an enemy-like behavior comes up, place it in the category of the enemy's camp. Leave it there. Don't agree with anything in the enemy's arsenal. Learning to recognize a secretive enemy thought or statement will help to free oneself of it. The first step is to recognize it; the second step is to categorize it, and the final step is to leave it there.

One of the enemy's weapons is to take something said innocently and distort it. It happened rampantly to me before each of my estrangements with my mother and daughter. It's recognizable because distortion and chaos ensues when someone misinterprets another's intentions. One will be fully unaware until an accuser hurls words or actions back completely twisted. Have you ever asked, "Where did that come from?" in response to these words? Suddenly the twisting of words and actions land you in the land of unworthy, not good enough, or a bad person. Soon, even personally you may be agreeing with the enemy if you do not categorize this plotting directive. Remind yourself you are worthy; you are good enough; you are valuable and let those twisted words fall flat.

I have observed instances where others became estranged or have had heated outbursts stemming from someone distorting multiple truths in some way. It is almost like the person accusing was looking for something wrong in the one they accused. In cases where I had witnessed this personally and fervently praying next to women who could not comprehend why their family was falling apart, each of us had been accused of multiple minuscule things. From my experience it is best if you take notice, fully hold your peace, and respond with as much compassion as possible because there could be something sinister under it all that hasn't been exposed yet.

Take your focus off the accusing words and look for a root cause. In many of these cases, the small multiple accusations serve to mask a big sinister bomb about to explode from the accuser and his or her agitators. An accuser trying to hide and hold on to an addiction in secret will always agree with the enemy camp of secret addictions. In cases like this, know that the accuser is the one who has to categorize his or her actions in the rightful kingdom where addictions thrive. The serenity prayer is your best friend in a moment like this.

The twisting of words with my own estrangements propelled me to set up a healthy practice to ensure my thoughts were not twisted with anyone. If I now hear someone say something with a tonality that can be twisted, I try to take note and carefully say, "What did you just say, because the way you said it may be twisted in a way you never meant? What did you mean? Could you help me to understand?"

Often while out with friends, a silly joke or situation will be a part of jest. Because of my own experience with the twisting of words, when I notice this I will purposely point out, "Please, no one twist that joke or jest. It did not mean anything sinister or bad. It is only silly; do not make it a cloudy monstrosity." What I find most interesting when I do this, all involved look surprised and then in full agreement nod their heads like "Yeah someone could twist it. I will not."

As more healthy behavior becomes our norm, a person who has been a part of blaming and shaming within your circles may still continue. What will be different is your healthy patterns will gain maturity. You will be more alert and secure. You will start to see others' unhealthy behaviors as a harbinger to their own friction to come. Their own gaslighting, deflecting, projecting and more may falsely alleviate the shame within them caused by their own hidden conscience, but you will be able to hold our peace.

When the real root of conflict is exposed it is a massive relief that the pain was due to something you could have never have known or suspected. The freedom in knowing you were on the receiving end of someone else's sinister little secret is a relief. It will be painful, but it will be a relief.

When you realize that your accusers were accusing because you were a constant reminder of their own hidden secrets, recall the serenity prayer. Remember that it is/was a situation for someone else to find their own resolve.

Now, I will write out an instance like any of the above situations. If I find a sinister element on my list, I mark it out with a big X. This is my way of giving the sinister camp back its X; I'm done with it. I let it fall flat; it is not welcome in my personal or cultural kingdom of clarity and love.

The next kingdom that I like to focus on is the personal kingdom. Getting right with oneself is when we alone are in our own way, in our own head, or in need of freedom from fallacy thoughts that we see as absolutes. Look in the mirror; there one will find the Kingdom of Self. While you are there, grab your thoughts and ask, "Is this an orphan thought? Is this a thought that is not who I want to be?" This practice helps us to recognize that in our personal alone time, we may be tempted to agree with something we are not.

We are not orphans. Psalms 68:5 was written with our name on it! "Father of the fatherless and protector of widows is God in his holy habitation," Psalms 68:5. Write your name in place of "fatherless" and "widows." Say it out loud as many times as you need to while looking at yourself in the mirror. My name reads like "Father of Jodi LaRae Cunningham and of mine is God in his holy habitation," Psalms 68:5. Just writing this made me feel more alert, and light. There is freedom in using Scripture; it covers each of the three kingdoms, so use it to strengthen your own personal Kingdom of Self.

In the Kingdom of Self, the best outcome for an issue is when it lies within, and we know it. Here is where and when we recognize we are creating limited space for ourselves. Here we decide enough is enough. We are in charge. Here we are going to discipline ourselves to do our grief work, drop our expectations, stay the course, take personal responsibility, and decide to approach life from a place of a learning mindset.

When we are right with ourselves, here we will relish and enjoy our self-improvement. Others will benefit naturally from our self-resolve and inner peace. When the issue lies within, we can tackle it with the help of a loving community, a trained professional, and/or coping skills to recognize that our fallacy thoughts need to be replaced with truth and hope. We begin to experience the road towards health and safety, where peaceful moments multiply when we get right with ourselves. Here we learn that grieving is of great value because it proves that we have and can love. We can love and we are lovable. Growing through our grief is proof we were navigating the personal self-kingdom well.

Twelve-step programs like Celebrate Recovery are ideal for being in a community while exploring one's own personal areas to improve or simply to be aware of. Here in Las Vegas, Churches hold many of the 12-step programs. Central Church in Henderson, from the pulpit promotes going to Celebrate

Recovery even if one does not have alcohol or drug addictions. Recovery is for all people who have habits, hurts, and hang ups. Notice, that covers all of us.

In a Celebrate Recovery class at Central church in Henderson, thousands of people go into a large meeting with a speaker and music. These meetings end with the Serenity Prayer and are followed up with smaller groups for drug addictions, alcohol addictions, enablers, and codependents. In each class there are rules to what one can say and one cannot say. Each person speaks within a time set for them. During this time, people are only allowed to speak about themselves personally. It is a moment to practice self-work, but in a group that encourages self work. The bravest people I've ever met are the ones getting right with themselves at a 12-step. Learning to recognize and categorize our own habits, hurts, and hang ups truly is a goal worth pursuing.

Ideally, when the root cause of a habit, hang up or hurt is exposed within its respective kingdom, it becomes possible to identify the source of trouble and initiate a process of letting go for the purpose of rebuilding and starting fresh. Whoever can recognize; forgive fallacy thoughts; and prioritize love, kindness, gentleness, and understanding will find solace, even if they stand alone. However, if we are not aware of where the turbulent issues originate, chaos takes center stage eventually in every kingdom. When real solutions remain elusive, blame and shame persist.

What we do not know, nor what we did not cause, we cannot solve. It isn't until we start looking through the lenses of the personal, cultural, and sinister that we can remove, release, and set ourselves free from the pressures within each one that are keeping us from our full potential.

We want to grow to our full potential through the personal and cultural kingdoms. Imagine our growth is like the rising of dough from a yeast recipe. After a few hours, we lift the towel and see the dough has grown so much that the bowl has no room for anything else. If we are growing in great practices like recognizing and organizing our personal growth and loving our communities, then like the risen dough our growth is fully expanding too.

What grew out of Dr. Shelly Hogan's doctoral studies was the inception of E5 Life Strategies. Dr. Hogan has been instrumental in expanding its reach and assisting numerous individuals in overcoming their challenges, specifically in the "remember when" moments of their lives. She achieves this by breaking down those moments into smaller pieces and assigning them to their respective kingdoms.

It is noteworthy that all these kingdoms are subordinate to God's Kingdom, which governs our existence here on Earth. Until we find ourselves fully in God's Kingdom here on Earth, interacting kindly with one another personally and culturally takes skill, practice, and alertness.

Categorizing an event or an action into a kingdom is a way to chunk down or hone in to discover the core of our actions in a particular moment. Ask yourself questions like, "What was influencing my actions? Was it me alone? Was it the culture I was in? If I was harming others or myself was there a sinister influence I was in agreement with?" For me, this practice has been valuable to "get out of my head" and see things for what they were or what they were not. This also helps me to forgive, let go and reset.

Considering ourselves, we can imagine a kingdom that revolves around our personal desires and physical needs. This personal kingdom entails solely focusing on ourselves and contemplating our own needs, wants, hopes, and desires without any external cultural influence. A concrete example that illustrates this concept is when we decide to purchase a new pair of running shoes exclusively for our use. We believe that these new shoes will enhance our running experience and prioritize taking care of our own body.

The personal kingdom can be culturally influenced and will change the motivation behind purchasing new shoes or pursuing a new hobby. For example, if we are buying new shoes for our running hobby and we are aware that the top runners only wear a specific brand of shoes, we might choose to purchase that brand solely because it is endorsed by the best runners. The cultural influence of these top runners wearing those shoes suggests that wearing them may lead to our best performance while running. This exemplifies how culture can influence personal choices.

In this scenario, the decision to buy new running shoes becomes part of the larger cultural group of runners. The act of purchasing running shoes now becomes a personal choice influenced by the culture surrounding running. Ultimately, this intertwining relationship between personal preferences and cultural influences creates a mutually influential dynamic within one's own personal kingdom and those of others.

In the cultural kingdom, we have families, towns, cities, countries, schools, hospitals, police officers, fire departments, sports leagues, the arts and much more. Within these parts of our world, certain countries like the USA are characterized by a strong sense of independence and a preference for doing things our own way. A beloved song in the United States that embodies this attitude is "I did it "My Way" by Frank Sinatra.

On the other hand, in places like Asia, respect for family plays a significant role and often takes precedence over individual desires. This is often labeled as a shame and honor culture. Here a culture's honor is more important than an individual's desire to make life choices that may cause dishonor for the family. Arranged marriages and working for the family business is often a norm in cultures that prioritizes the culture above an individual.

A simple illustration that I witnessed of how cultures perceive the same situation differently happened during an adult Bible study session I attended in NYC. During a group discussion, a male participant from Chicago shared his excitement about his Brazilian wife's newfound interest in riding a bicycle. Being an avid cyclist himself, he had been waiting for this moment for 30 years since they got married for her to say, "I would love to bike ride with you." He was ecstatic and he wanted to give her the finest bike available. Thus, he diligently searched for and extensively discussed various options with her for her new bicycle.

Sometime during the time they were shopping for bicycles, they attended a party. They encountered a passionate Iron Man participant. The wife engaged in a conversation with this professional athlete regarding which bike to purchase. When her husband realized that she was talking to the top-tier cyclist, he couldn't help but feel betrayed by her interest in Iron Man. This encounter left him feeling frustrated and somewhat jealous of their interaction. She failed to realize that her newfound interest in bike riding with her husband was actually his personal dream: to ride together, just the two of them. Now, not only had she received different advice from someone else about a bicycle, it was advice from a skilled cyclist, Iron Man.

As the huddle of bible study attendees listened to the husband tell this story, a man from China piped up and said to him, "What is the big deal? Your wife was just wanting to be educated. She was just speaking about bicycles and getting more knowledge on the best bicycle. That seems rational to me."

Wow! The man from Chicago was incredibly frustrated—to the point where he seemed ready to explode. The Chinese man, on the other hand, sat there bewildered, not understanding what was happening. The rest of us felt uneasy because we didn't know if things would escalate beyond just words being exchanged.

The independent American man longed for a romantic experience with his wife— a date where they could shop for bicycles together, just the two of them. He wanted to be her companion and someone she could look up to in finding the perfect bike that he knew she would adore. However, Iron Man intervened smoothly and had her attentively listen to every detail about which bike to choose.

Inside of me, I wondered at the time if Iron Man looked as good as the "I can't believe it's not butter" man. Don't worry, that was a joke; don't twist my joke; I promise I won't run off with the butter man. However, I do like butter, ha!

Meanwhile, the man from China approached the situation with logical thinking of why not ask the most skilled person? On the other hand, the American man approached it more creatively and pictorially from his hopes and dream finally coming true of him and his wife enjoying wonderful morning rides to the park before sunset. Iron Man had no place in his dream.

This incident sheds light on cultural differences and their impact on our personal perceptions when it comes to simple tasks like choosing a bike or fulfilling complex roles such as being a provider, hero, and gift-giver to a wife.

When examining the personal and cultural kingdoms, it is important to consider various factors that can influence each other. Additionally, one must be mindful of the enemy's kingdom, which has the potential to impact both the personal and cultural kingdoms unless precautions are taken to prevent manipulation from occurring.

The sinister kingdom not only harms individuals but also the cultures it becomes a part of. Let's again take the simple example of buying running shoes. If someone purchases new running shoes solely to gain popularity among other runners, this can be considered sinister. The act becomes sinister because the intention behind buying the shoes was not solely to enhance one's performance and add value to the race, but rather to fit in and be well-liked. In this case, good sportsmanship takes a backseat and fitting in becomes the primary motivation. Perhaps the desire to fit in with top runners leads to an invitation to their exclusive clubs or helps improve one's social standing among others. However, instead of focusing on becoming better at a sport one is passionate about, one might end up trying too hard to impress others and neglect their own growth and development, not only on the running field, but also in their business world too. Those shoes in a way become an idol.

When our personal or physical desires clash or ignite with the norms of those we are around, no matter how hard we try to address and correct our behavior, finding inner balance can become a struggle. Conflict can persist under the sinister kingdom like an open wound. I have personally experienced minor instances where I later discovered that the sinister kingdom was influencing the cultural kingdom around me. It seemed that no matter what I did, it was always considered wrong. Whether it was something as simple as pressing a button in an elevator or fastening my seat belt promptly enough, nothing seemed to satisfy this person's expectations. Even when I made efforts to improve in these areas, it didn't seem to matter to them; they continued to remind me of my shortcomings. The truth was, it wasn't actually the perception of me that bothered them, it was the fact I no longer fit into the social class they preferred being with. In that case, the sinister was happy to tempt and agitate.

I've attended churches where they feed the homeless after services. There, people who attend services are both homeless and not homeless. Learning how to show grace and kindness between these two social classes is a process practiced. It's beautiful. However, when the two social classes clash, people between the two groups are cold and sneer at one another. A verbal argument may ensue and possibly escalate. It is almost always an issue of perceived social status. Can you guess which kingdoms this example falls in?

Estrangement doesn't occur without any reason. It can often serve as a shield for innocent individuals involved, especially if an enemy has infiltrated their own personal and cultural kingdoms. When malevolent influences are allowed to thrive, estrangement can actually protect us. It can offer us time, solitude and rest to heal from what was or was not going on in each person's Kingdom of Self and Kingdom of Culture.

Many of us who experience estrangement were aware that there was something happening within ourselves and our families that we just could not fully work through. Each person involved within their own personal and cultural kingdom was unclear on all that they could not change, nor did they have the courage to change all that they could. Let's make the most of our estrangement now by taking the time to learn to categorize what we do know, change what we can, and accept what we cannot change.

*Journal**

1. 1.Put a heading on a paper: "THE KINGDOM OF GOD Proverbs 16:1-9." Below this write out the kingdom of self, others and the enemy. Categorize.
2. Write out what you actually need in your personal kingdom vs. your wants.
3. 3.Practice solitude in your personal time, savoring the moments in quiet time to rest and feel peace.

4. In your cultural kingdom, practice neutral tonality communication and compassion towards others.

5. * Dr. Shelly Hogan did a video for us in our Skool Membership Classroom: www.skool.com Estrangement, Moms&Daughters

Chapter 5

The ACE Trauma Test with Helpful Acknowledgments From Dr. Alfonso Gilbert and the Emotional Organ Chart.

This chapter is a direct paraphrasing of my lecture notes from Grand Canyon University with Dr. Gilbert in 2021, as well as the online Zoom meeting we had on December 26, 2023. The ACE test questions are at the end of this chapter. I have a score of 7 and knowing this score has helped me to be aware of my own emotions and personal health.

The ACE traumas may or may not be experiences you have personally gone through. Still, we can gain insight into how unprocessed trauma, if not dealt with, halts healing and growth. Individuals who respond to life experiences in a detached, apathetic manner or in an obsessive way may have unhealed childhood trauma that has blocked their own brain pathways from fully experiencing joy with self and others.

The ACE test represents adverse childhood experiences, which may affect the way a mother and daughter interact with one another. If neither the mother nor the daughter have experienced any trauma, it is probable that individuals who have daily influence amongst them throughout the day might have had their own unresolved childhood trauma. These individuals could be a spouse, an employer, a teacher, or a friend who may react in ways that are influenced by their own past traumas.

Most of us are familiar with the concept of helicopter parenting, which can manifest as a hyper-vigilant approach in which parents try to constantly protect their child. This can lead to the child feeling suffocated or controlled. On the other hand, there are parents who may habitually shut down emotionally, even when they are physically present but emotionally unavailable. As a result, they struggle to provide supportive responses that help their child feel comforted during times of distress. Trauma that lingers in the body can play out either way. Often, we find ourselves unaware of the reasons behind our reactions or inactions that provoke responses from individuals carrying unresolved traumas.

It is essential to acknowledge that our past can act as a significant obstacle when it comes to mourning events, moments, or even the loss of loved ones. Trauma barriers can hinder us from embarking on a healthy journey in life or being a safe person for someone even when we try to be. A helicopter mother's ultimate desire is for her child to never experience grief, but ironically, it tends to be the very thing we fail to teach them how to work through. Often, helicopter mothers tend to distract themselves by engaging in various activities in order to avoid any form of grieving, especially if it stirs up emotions linked with past traumas.

The ACE Research and Impact of Childhood Trauma study monitored a group of 17,000 individuals from the average age of 57 for 20 years(Gilbert, 2023). The study revealed ten most prevalent childhood traumas that became evident before the age of 18. The participants were then followed until they reached the age of 80. The findings clearly demonstrated that even a single trauma experienced during childhood has the potential to severely disrupt adult life. Furthermore, individuals who encountered four traumas faced significantly elevated risks of depression, suicidal tendencies, addiction, and health complications.

If these traumas were not resolved, healed, or treated, they had the potential to trigger an individual in a manner that would cause them to overreact or perceive even the simplest things as significant threats. Professions like that of a police officer may develop a hyper-vigilant mindset that constantly searches for potential dangers. As part of their training, police officers are taught coping mechanisms to aid them in maintaining a healthy balance between their personal and professional lives while dealing with frequent threats and trauma. However, children who carry traumas into adulthood may not possess the knowledge of healthy coping skills that police officers receive.

An adult who has experienced one or more ACE traumas, but has never processed them, may experience emotional numbness and engage in addictive behaviors or violence. This state can be referred to as dissociation from one's body and mind.

Dr. Gilbert conducted research for his doctoral degree comparing first-generational pastors to second-generational pastors as they lived out their calling in the Church. The evidence he discovered was remarkably clear: first-generation pastors who came from families where one or more ACE traumas occurred were significantly different from second-generation pastors who were raised by parents without ACE traumas in their family background.

With his findings Dr. Gilbert also found four steps towards healing trauma that could aid pastors who came from traumatic backgrounds to heal and assist others on their own healing journey. The pastors who had adverse childhood traumas could relate to almost 100% of their church congregations, with traumas being the shared experiences.

Dr. Gilbert has outlined a series of steps for healing and reprocessing past traumas:

1. Discover a community that can provide you with support. By creating an environment where you feel emotionally and physically secure, you can rebuild the trust that has been weakened by past trauma.
2. Give yourself the chance to experience a fresh community that can nurture the growth of hope, purpose, and imagination within you once more. Often, it is in the depths of our right brain where trauma resides, making it difficult for us to perceive hope, purpose, and imagination. A healing community will wholeheartedly believe in you and provide support in rekindling your dreams and imagination.
3. Express your trauma by going through a process of grieving. Instead of disconnecting from it,

acknowledge the pain. Acknowledging the pain will enable you to heal as you are aware of what exactly you are healing from. Identify the specific emotion that you are experiencing; recognize it, and learn to acknowledge its presence.

4. Start the process of retraining yourself in something new. By learning a fresh activity, you can reconstruct the neural pathways that have been hindered by trauma. Explore an unfamiliar hiking trail; discover the art of fishing; master sewing techniques, or delve into a foreign language. Embrace these novel experiences, and as you do so, you will experience a greater sense of achievement and realize that it is indeed possible to continue learning, enjoy life, and contribute to others' happiness. For instance, if you learn how to play the piano, you can delight someone with a birthday song.

After completing our video meeting, which you can find on our Skool.com community called Estrangement, Moms&Daughters, there was one question that deeply echoed in my being. It specifically concerned mothers or daughters who had caused estrangement due to their experiences with childhood trauma and their relationships. I wondered about the type of encouragement that Dr. Gilbert had for them in this situation, where forgiving oneself feels like an overwhelming and almost impossible burden.

Dr. Gilbert himself experienced seven traumatic events and acknowledged making regrettable choices in his earlier adult life. He also recognized that his mother's decisions were influenced by her own childhood trauma. As a pastor raising children, he became aware of the impact of unresolved childhood trauma on his own decision making, leading to feelings of regret.

Dr. Gilbert emphasized that forgiving oneself for past actions is challenging no matter how much faith one has or does not have. It is hard for everyone. It is essential to confront forgiving oneself with vulnerability in order to overcome shame and regret. Becoming a safe and healed person is crucial in this journey of forgiving oneself. It is a milestone of courage and safety for self and others to begin the steps of forgiving. It is possible to find healing within even amidst estrangement by following the four steps mentioned above and openly expressing vulnerability. This demonstrates empathy for others' feelings caused by our actions or inactions. To admit and forgive oneself can be like drawing a figurative line in the sand and stepping over it. Then follow it up with the four steps above.

As we ponder on the traumas that confine our emotions, in this second part of this chapter, I aim to illustrate how emotions that remain unprocessed and unresolved can become trapped within our bodies, often without us realizing it. Moreover, I will show how reprocessing a trapped emotion is possible. This task is not simple, yet with practice, one can improve and eventually experience a noticeable transformation.

As we learn to observe our emotions with thoughtfulness, we will experience a sense of relief in our bodies when we realize that we have the power to overcome and let go. Healing from deep-rooted emotions that have been trapped within us since childhood is possible with the support of a community, especially with the guidance of a personal counselor. Additionally, it can aid in healing from the reactions of individuals who may have responded to random incidents based on their own unresolved trauma.

Experiencing estrangement is incredibly painful, but it is possible to heal and move forward on your own side. When we confront our trapped emotions in the mirror, we acknowledge them, process them, and release them. There is no need for these emotions to linger and add to new situations where they simply pile on top of one another. Instead, we recognize that we have felt these emotions before, dealt with them, and moved on from them. Lasting resolution can occur—at least on our side. And when new problems arise, we have the ability to reset ourselves by processing past emotions, knowing that they have been healed. We can then heal and reset again for the new challenges that come our way.

The following emotions and organs are from an emotional chart that Audrey Miesner of Love Married Life gave me from my own personal counseling. You may look up other emotional charts or emotional mapping online and find a plethora of information. These emotions hold immense power and can burden our bodies. I hope this provides you with the courage to begin the healing process, as your body doesn't need to be held captive by past trauma.

When you feel one of these emotions, look at the body part that is connected to the stressful emotion. Then try and remember the first time you felt that emotion. See the very moment. See what you were doing. See what was going on. Tell your younger self, you made it. You are older and wiser. You do not have to ever return to that moment. This time your adult self is helping you now to know you did your best. Today you are where you should be. Thank your young self for doing your best.

Heart and small intestines will feel:

- Abandonment, betrayal, embarrassment, forlornness,heartache, panic, sadness, sorrow, insecurity, vulnerability (no boundaries)
- Lost love, over excitement, unreceived love, unforgiveness

Spleen and stomach:

- Anxiety, deprivation, despair, disappointment, disgust, dissatisfaction, emptiness, failure, greed, nausea, nervousness, mania
- Hopelessness, pensiveness, lack of control, low self-esteem

Lungs and large intestines:

- Confusion, contempt, disdain, grief, guilt, happiness, intolerance, judgment, justice, pride, sadness, scorn
- Defensiveness, self-abuse, self-hatred, low self-worth, unhappiness, unworthiness, weepiness, worthlessness

Liver and bladder:

- Anger, bitterness, frustration, hatred, rage, resentment, stress
- Explosiveness, fury, wrath, taken for granted, indecisiveness.

Kidney and bladder:

- Sexual insecurity, sexual indecision, blame, dread, horror, irritation, restlessness, frustration, impatience, conflict, invalidated, creative security, feebleness, shock

Pericardium and triple burner:

- Despondency, depression, humiliation, jealousy, longing, lust, melancholiness, sexuality, remorse, shame, solitude, stubbornness, tension
- Overwhelmingness, heaviness, hopelessness, double mindedness, loneliness,

These emotions are universal and can be experienced by anyone at some point in their life. Many of us carry these emotions with us every day, residing within us on an organ, ready to remind us of its presence whenever it is triggered. When these emotions are ignored and not properly addressed for healing, growth, maturity, and forgiveness, they may unexpectedly spill out onto someone who is unaware of what just happened. By recalling an experience that triggered a suppressed emotion, it may become evident how important it is to confront and deal with these emotions.

An emotion like double mindedness may appear so much that your friends may tell you, "You always change your mind and I can never count on you." Double mindedness comes from a deep hopelessness that can affect your heart. I carried hopelessness in my heart way into my forties from adults changing their minds about very important moments. Fortunately, I was asked in my forties by a very interesting person I met, "Jodi, do you find that you have double-mindedness when you make decisions? Have you found that you may wait a long time to make a decision, but after so many months you always make the same decision you originally made?" From that moment, I started to trust myself and let go of the hopeless experiences I had that stemmed from other people changing their mind at the last minute as early as when I was six years old.

The emotional feeling of creative insecurity can affect the kidneys and the bladder. When I think of how my creativity was scrutinized by a teacher, I also remember always wanting to go to the bathroom. I think it was just to hide out, honestly. I remember a history teacher told me that my map was not colored well enough to receive a grade better than a "B." He then went on to show the class how an "A+" map looked. The only difference was my map was done using light pressure on a crayon, while the other was done using a lot of pressure. The "A+" map colors were heavy and dark. We both colored in the map fully; just the pressure made a difference? I have much younger memories of creative insecurity, but in the seventh grade this one stuck out to me as an earlier experience that gave me the same emotion that was awaiting upon my organs already.

Simple events like this can feel magnitudinous to a child. Sometimes these moments can elicit deep emotional wounds, especially if these emotions are set atop past experiences that did not have a good outcome. These emotions are in us to learn how to heal from them. If you feel one of these emotions, it is a good idea to try and remember when you felt them the very first time. Your adult self now, is able to help your younger self. As we learn to heal, we can realize how we have contributed to how others have felt because of us directly.

Part of assuming personal responsibility and acknowledging the impact we have on others is being able to apologize for causing others negative feelings, even if we were unaware of it. Upon reflection, perhaps these emotions were also a result of something unresolved within others. For me, if creative insecurity was still stuck in me, I would have a very hard time being a writer or a communicator of very challenging topics, like estrangement.

Perhaps we may not have fully grasped our true feelings or those of others. Even worse, we may have been unaware of how we made others feel and yet we continued to act in a harmful manner. In situations like these, it becomes crucial for us to embrace vulnerability, take responsibility, and acknowledge our actions by saying "Yes, I did that. I deeply regret it. I commit to never repeating such behavior again because I will actively work on processing those emotions within myself and liberate myself from them."

Through self-reflection, I have come to understand that there are aspects of my life for which I bear sole responsibility and fault. However, it was not until my relationship with my adult daughter became strained, and she expressed a preference for a life without me, that I truly grasped the extent of the harm I had unknowingly caused her.

Recognizing this, I have been diligently working through these issues on my own using an emotional chart. It is highly probable that any humiliation I experienced during my own childhood inadvertently manifested in ways that caused my daughter to feel humiliated by either my actions or lack thereof at some point. As I examine an emotional organ mapping chart, I discover lingering emotions within myself. It is not difficult for me to recognize that my own actions may have caused someone else to experience a similar emotion.

As an adult woman, I experienced a seven-year estrangement from my own mother. Unfortunately, we find ourselves in the same predicament once again, realizing that both instances were caused by the same underlying issue which triggered unresolved emotions that were never processed on both sides. While I have managed to resolve my side of my emotions, true reconciliation between us can only be achieved if both parties address and release their trapped emotions. We can never push the other person to resolve; we can only resolve within ourselves on our own side. Then we can have genuine compassion over the lingering issues that were caused by circumstances outside of our control.

With Dr. Gilbert's research on ACE trauma and the emotional chart, we have the ability to process emotions, and to sow seeds of positivity and hope within ourselves and others. It is not easy, but it is possible, especially with a community. We are inherently valuable. We have brought forth human life in the form of our daughters. It is a truly extraordinary and profound mystery! Mothers teach their daughters, who in turn pass on this knowledge to their own daughters. Together, we can accomplish new things, and even if we encounter failure, we can take solace in knowing that we tried our best without being burdened by suppressed emotions from our past. This allows us to find peace within ourselves.

Start now; start here. Keep going. I've been working on this since 2020 and I'm still finding emotions that I have to reprocess. I'm grateful to know the emotions, to know how far to look for them in my past and release myself from them with forgiveness and full restoration of my part.

The ACE Trauma Questions are from NPR [NPR.org. "Take the Ace Quiz—And Learn What it Does and Doesn't Mean." [March 2, 2015, last date viewed Feb. 16, 2024, https://www.npr.org/sections/health-shots/2015/03/02/387007941/take-the-ace-quiz-and-learn-what-it-does-and-doesnt-mean].

If you have one or more of these traumas, you can heal and you can recognize how they may affect your adult behavior in many life situations. The first part of knowing how to overcome and how to cope, is to know that you can.

1. Before your 18th birthday, did a parent or other adult in the household often or very often swear at you, insult you, put you down, or humiliate you, or act in a way that made you afraid that you might be physically hurt?

2. Before your 18th birthday, did a parent or other adult in the household often or very often push, grab, slap,

or throw something at you, or ever hit you so hard that you had marks or were injured?

3. Before your 18th birthday, did an adult or person at least five years older than you ever touch or fondle you or have you touch their body in a sexual way, or attempt to or actually have oral, anal, or vaginal intercourse with you?

4. Before your 18th birthday, did you often or very often feel that no one in your family loved you or thought you were important or special, or that your family didn't look out for each other, feel close to each other, or support each other?

5. Before your 18th birthday, did you often or very often feel that you didn't have enough to eat, had to wear dirty clothes, and had no one to protect you, or your parents were too drunk or high to take care of you or take you to the doctor if you needed it?

6. Before your 18th birthday, was a biological parent ever lost to you through divorce, abandonment, or other reason?

7. Before your 18th birthday, was your mother or stepmother often or very often pushed, grabbed, slapped, or had something thrown at her, or sometimes, often, or very often kicked, bitten, hit with a fist, or hit with something hard, or ever repeatedly hit over at least a few minutes or threatened with a gun or knife?

8. Before your 18th birthday, did you live with anyone who was a problem drinker or alcoholic, or who used street drugs?

9. Before your 18th birthday, was a household member depressed or mentally ill, or did a household member attempt suicide?

10. Before your 18th birthday, did a household member go to prison?

Chapter 6

Communication Goals for a Life of Security and Value.**

This chapter on communication goals is derived from my time spent with Bob and Audrey Meisner, who are the creators of Love Married Life. In 2020, I embarked on a healing journey with both of them. You can obtain a copy of Audrey and Bob Meisner's booklet, My Communication Goals, from their website: www.lovemarriedlife.com. The booklet is available as a digital eBook in the resources section. It provides a clear outline of communication goals such as feeling safe, liked, right, and in control. The majority of the following is direct paraphrasing from my Zoom meeting with Bob that you may find inside of our classroom on www.skool.com Estrangement, Moms&Daughters.

The Communication Goals were developed as a means to achieve a beneficial resolution in interpersonal communication. Without acknowledging our own communication goals, which are rooted in our unique ways of perceiving ourselves and others, we may unintentionally approach communication with fear rather than love. Knowing the four communication goals are especially helpful in developing deeper bonds.

Communication goals are not meant to be better than each other, but based on one's own natural feelings. People will have a natural way they like to communicate over another. In the chapter on kingdoms, the Kingdom of Self is about becoming right with yourself. Understanding your primary and secondary communication objectives will not only provide you with self-awareness but also enable you to cultivate a harmonious relationship, both within yourself and with others.

If we do not know our communication goals we will not feel we have been heard. We will not feel that we are valued, or loved. A communication goal in itself is to know that what we said was important to the listener as much as it is to oneself. If one wishes to be a better communicator, it is essential to understand one's top-two most-felt goals of being liked, right, safe, or controlled.

The liked, right, safe or controlled will fall in an order from top to bottom. The primary choices for each person are the top two, while the less important ones for that person are the bottom two. If two people in a conversation each like to feel liked and safe as a goal, there is a high probability that their communication will result in them feeling secure, appreciated, and esteemed. If two people where one has a top goal of right and the other has a top goal of safe, unless they understand this, the chances of the simplest personal questions will agitate, even in a blissful environment.

It is quite difficult when we have a conversation with someone and we cannot express what we would like to share. We walk away feeling they do not value us or our opinion. One of my top goals is to feel safe. In the past if I felt someone was doing something where I knew it was unsafe or they were trying to lead my child down a path of an unsafe consequence, this momma turned into a grizzly momma bear. Now, because I know safety is an important goal for me specifically, I now do what I can to create a safe place for myself and others if possible. When I cannot, I lean on the Serenity Prayer.

Someone who wants to feel control, wants to feel comfortable knowing how something will work out with their input. If a person who loves control first has their contribution ignored, they may feel that they do not fit into a conversation. Contrasting this with a safe, driven person who may not want to continuously cover details; the control person needs to know there is a time and a place to discuss details for clarity and planning with a person whose first communication goal is safety.

When we are secure in ourselves, we can be with another in their differences. Have you ever been told you are too sensitive as you are crying and pouring your heart out because you have to share something you don't want to share with your mother or your daughter? If you were being called oversensitive, the chances are both of you were insecure in your own communication goals.

Someone secure can understand how to absorb someone else's different communication goal, especially when they wish to share news no one wants to talk about. True sensitivity is connecting with someone in their pain, even if one doesn't agree with them. Sensitivity is not just toning down your voice, it is actually hearing others so they know you heard them. You understand how they feel. You are OK not feeling like them or thinking like them, but you understand and can empathize with what they are thinking and feeling.

It can be difficult to get your child to comprehend what you are saying is important. It can also be difficult letting your mom know how she makes you feel or how you are feeling. In cases like this each of you are struggling to be heard. Understanding both mom's and daughter's communication objective will ensure that both benefit from a conversation and feel heard.

Prior to meeting Bob and Audrey I had little understanding of how individuals tend to experience certain emotions more strongly based on their natural disposition of right, control, safe or liked. Worse, I was totally out of touch with my own natural communication goal that I preferred for myself. In my past, I had blindly altered my own natural communication goals to shape my marriage and my role as a mother and a daughter.

Before each of my estrangements, my communication goals were right, controlled, liked and safe. To my surprise, after taking the communication goals test I realized naturally I enjoyed the communication goals of being safe, liked, right and controlled. My top two natural dispositions were safe and liked. This was the complete opposite of how I was living! In a way, I had estranged from my natural self!

How did this happen? Life happened to me. I had been married to a military man where every one-to-two years we had to move. I had to be right about how each move would be organized and more. After 33 years of marriage, I had 33 address changes. Then, I knew as we moved people would not like us right away because we were newcomers and they would have to get to know us. I also knew that being safe enough to share my life with non-military people would not fully ever be understood. So being liked and safe for me in that lifestyle was something I just had to forgo, so I thought.

I also grew up in a construction ranching family, where ensuring the successful completion of construction tasks and performing labor jobs correctly was paramount. It had to be done right and the bottom line had to be controlled. This was because we built homes for people to live in, and it was crucial to prioritize their safety and satisfaction. However, merely being safe and well-liked in the construction industry was insufficient when sales were low. Fear often ruled daily life because profit and control of a build had to be right as our family's livelihood depended on it.

When I realized that my two natural communication goals were safe and liked, I realized my true whole person felt best communicating my goals inside of the emotions of safe and liked. It was a relief that inside of any environment, I could be secure communicating naturally instead of becoming my environment.

Realizing this, I began recognizing how little moments of my past where my goals of safe and liked would emerge freely. I loved hospitality. I loved organizing a party, a benefit, or even a luncheon where everyone liked the food, the company and the friendship. I also noticed that my son and daughter also liked to feel safe. When we would work on something to make everyone feel welcomed and a plan would come together well, I remember we were almost completely in sync. Before the estrangement, I was pushing the goal of right and controlled because I thought that was expected of me. When each needed me to care about what made both feel safe to heal a poor situation, we were as opposite as the south and north poles.

Ignoring my natural disposition eventually landed me in Bob and Audrey's office wondering how my whole life had been destroyed and stolen in front of my eyes. I was facing estrangement, known betrayals of the worst kind, and the reality of very cruel intentions from those I never should have allowed to shape me. Had I not looked deeply into how I actually enjoyed feeling, I could still be on a course that simply was never for me.

As I started seeing myself more clearly, shedding off *who I wasn't* was welcomed. Now, in my natural state, in a session I said, "Audrey, naturally I like to feel safe by helping and listening to others. I like to feel liked because I love giving hope and happiness. Instead, somehow I became my environment! My environment was about being right out of fear of losing something. Loss of secrets, loss of income, loss of friendship and more. I still remember just sitting with myself realizing how I had got there. No wonder I made my children crazy when I would help, shout and be fully spun up with exhaustion. No one could hear my true self. How could they have been thankful? No one liked my helping; no one liked it at all. I don't think I did either.

Once I had journeyed through this revelation of my own actions, I looked at how these feeling categories landed on other people. The best part of my profound realization was that once and for all, I was done with being someone I was never supposed to be. The me that was acting out controlled and right, achieved and completed tasks often from a place of fear instead of the intention of valuing my own goal of feeling safe and liked. My efforts to move all those times and build out homes and remodels always left me with a feeling of just getting this done and getting through it.

Strangely, I did always wonder long before my estrangement why I did not get much joy out of our family successes and accomplishments. I was somewhat bored of it all. When I realized something was truly off after accomplishing some large achievements, I remember trying to figure out what I was missing: It was me. I thought I was attaining peace with every milestone finished, but instead my inner peace was elusive. Something was off, but I didn't know what it was. My natural feelings were completely rearranged and ignored.

When the four feelings of like, safe, right and control come into conflict with another, that is when we have a pressure situation that never seems to be solvable. Peace may seem elusive and not lasting when all these feelings are in a jumble. For instance, think about being around someone who just ticks you off. It seems that no matter what you try, the person who rubs you the wrong way seems to irritate something in you. You just cannot get anywhere with the other person. With this person, a two-person team sport would make you want to stop playing. When tapping into the four feelings of liked, safe, right, or control, one of you will value two feelings most and disvalue two feelings least. For instance, if person "A" values feeling liked and safe the most, but person "B" values these two feelings least, when it comes to problem solving, the situation will radically speed into a moment of pandemonium.

The same holds true if there is one person you just get! When you are around each other, you totally identify with what they think, how they feel and what they want. Your communication goals match like identical twins who really like each other. Two people with the same communication goals will create total harmony much sooner, even in chaos.

Since I learned of communication goals, I've thought of my daughter and my mom often. I wondered if I knew their four emotional goals in order. Were they living their natural emotional goals or were they living to appease their environment too? I did not know, and as yet, I don't know because we have never communicated on this deep level within this concept.

Each of these communication goals are a virtue as in a good gift, but each goal can be a vice when a person is motivated by fear instead of love. For me, learning how I was acting vs. how I actually felt before I ever even walked into adulthood was shocking, seeing how my feelings had such power within me. Instead of my feelings working well for me in a virtuous way, I was working against my own feelings which could flip my communications goals into a vice driven out of fear.

All virtues can slide into a vice. Like, safe, right and control are all virtues inside of love. When they slide into fear, they become a vice.

Who doesn't like being liked? The virtue of "liked" is attributed to the feeling that you just know all things will work out. You include others easily. You believe the best in another.

When "liked" turns into a vice, your desire to be liked may be so strong, you won't tell someone the truth about their actions. If the person is harming themselves or others, you keep silent or divert the problem to something else you can manage.

An example of this is a person who gets into a car with a drunk driver may care more about that person liking them than their own safety. Oddly, even though I had learned in my environment to feel right and controlled, because liked was my favored natural goal, I did get in a car with a drunk driver once. I knew I should not, but I was with a girlfriend and she did not want to make the man we were driving with angry, so we got in. We made it home but the whole way home; I was worried that my ex-husband would learn that I had ridden in the car with a drunk driver. I remember the relief I felt when we got to our destination, but I also felt glad that I had not made anyone mad at me. By having my goals flipped and then my natural goal of liked turned to a vice, I put myself in danger to please my friend.

Let's go over these goals in more detail:[3]

---

[3] https://ecourses.lovemarriedlife.com/my-communication-goals

Safe: The person who wants to feel "safe" in virtue, enjoys hearing people give detailed explanations or stories to their lives because it shows they truly trust one's honesty and vulnerability. When someone feels safe with you, you feel a loyalty or an appreciation that supersedes any other emotion. The vice of safety is that you may shut down and not even try to resolve anything because you may feel a threat to your own resolve, thoughts or preferences, and security. A needed conversation that makes one uncomfortable will take time for a person to open up to feel safe. If you would like to show love towards a person whose main goal is safe, show them a guarantee. Give them structure with known, kind boundaries.

Control: When you like to be in control, you may find yourself saying, I just don't trust other people. Someone who wants to be in control may always want to drive all the time, even with an experienced driver. Someone who wants to be in control will do the planning. When others notice the "controlled" emotion in someone, they know they make experiences special for them by keeping their best experiences in mind. This acknowledgment feels good for the controlled person. This kind of employee would love the boss letting them take over a task, have full control and be rewarded for it. The vice of control is one can appear bossy. To show a person with the goal of control first, let them drive! Show them appreciation as they give solutions. Recognize the great finished product of their work. When they organize a function, let them know you appreciated their attention to the details in accomplishing tasks.

Right: These people are experts in their field. They want their opinion to be valued. When all is done right, they feel good.

This person may lay out pieces to a swing set putting each piece together exactly as the directions say. A vice for this person is that when things are not done right, they may be inflexible. They may refuse to let some things slide and be joyful for being with someone if that someone doesn't do something precisely right . If you want to build up your relationship with a person whose number one goal is right, acknowledge what they do right by respecting their efforts to do so. Listen to their research on a topic they have deeply studied. Loyalty is a top priority because it is right.

Liked: Imagine a hostess everyone loves. The host of the party: who doesn't like parties and their host? Everyone at the party feels good and can open up easily because a liked person has gone out of their way to make sure they were happy. A like person hopes for the best. The vice for like is when a person withholds honesty for fear of not being liked. If you want to build a relationship with a liked person, help them to feel your love, by accepting them where they don't have to prove themselves or do anything for you. Be willing to communicate with them.

Download the free "My Communication Goals" from LoveMarriedLife.com. There you will find much more on this topic in detail.

Finally, what is true about relationships: if we don't understand how our mom/daughter likes to feel most, we will all have heightened stress especially in conflict.

When you think of yourself and another, put your top two relationship goals in order first. Then put your goals next to your daughter's/mother's if you know them. You will see similarities and conflicts appear almost instantly.

For instance,

Mom: Liked, Safe, Control, Right

Daughter: Right, Control, Safe, Liked

If mom likes to be liked first and wants to be right last, but daughter wants to be right first and liked last, any conflict is going to escalate. Even peaceful moments may feel as if it is the families' best interest to tiptoe around mom and daughter. Sound familiar?

Here is an example: Let's say the "elephant in the room" is cousin Joe who is known for drug use and mom has invited him to a Christmas dinner. That is a *big* elephant if no one else does drugs in the family. Possibly, some family members have covered for cousin Joe in the past. Maybe some are even taking care of Joe's children because he lost his children as a result of the drug use. Now this is quite a happy and fretful time if everyone has different relationship goals and are not secure in their goals.

Mom will very probably hug Joe and be glad he is there even if it is the last time he will be at a function because, let's all face it, drugs have a tendency to erase a person's function of caring about what may happen to them. Making Joe feel loved is a good thing and mom really wants Joe to like her.

Mom's daughter knows cousin Joe is walking a dangerous line and soon may take a wrong turn and harm himself or others. Out of fear for Joe, the daughter asks cousin Joe to get sober. Getting sober is a good thing, right? The daughter loves being right. Cousin Joe's drug use is wrong and not telling him is more wrong—right?!

Joe's reaction is definitely not from a place of security, but fear. Soon Joe is mad and leaves, making mom feel Joe doesn't like her. The daughter feels mom cares more about being liked than keeping Joe safe. Mom wanted daughter to let the holiday feel good for everyone, even Joe. Mom thinks her daughter does not appreciate how much effort she put into making everyone feel loved, even cousin Joe. The daughter thinks mom is selfish because she cared more about Joe rejecting her then Joe getting right with himself and others. Mom, daughter, and Joe all responded to the "elephant in the room" from a place of fear and not from a place of secure love.

From a place of love and value, mom could tell her daughter, "I want cousin Joe to feel welcomed and loved. I also know he needs to get right with himself and others. For today, let's just love him. If you like, we can invite him to stay longer when it is just us, and we can speak with him together." From a place of secure rightness, daughter could tell mom, "I know you want a nice Christmas dinner and I understand you want Joe to feel loved. After dinner could we both talk to Joe and see if he is willing to go into treatment?"

When our own natural feelings of communication goals are identified, we become secure in our own person. As we become secure in our own goals, we understand how our goals will help us to experience others. We should look at the virtues of our goals in love and recognize their tendency to fall into a vice of fear. Soon, we can decide we will operate only in love, not fear because we are clear on our goals and others. We will recognize the difference and know we are secure. From a place of security is where we can begin to offer forgiveness and apologize for our part in how we made others feel when the time comes.

Chapter 7

Sweet Resolve Inside of the Six Layers Apology

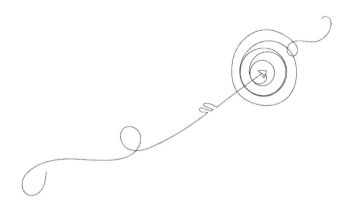

I was initially introduced to the concept of the six-layered apology by Bob and Audrey in early 2020. This apology process aims to deliver what Bob calls a "sweet resolve" between individuals who have experienced a breakdown in communication. Through a six-layer apology, we create a pathway for forgiveness, seek to be forgiven, and work towards reconciliation in order to achieve a state of sweet resolve. An apology that is truly acknowledged and accepted restores peace. It is an effective way to liberate ourselves and others from the pain that we all experience and understand from unresolved trauma or conflict.

Often, we hesitate to forgive or apologize until we fully comprehend the impact of our actions on others. Unless we comprehend this, it is difficult to understand them or their perception of us. By attempting to reconcile with those we have harmed, we are constructing a secure symbolic bridge that paves the way for a sweet resolve.

It is important to remember that everyone experiences pain: no one is exempt. Apologizing means recognizing and empathizing with someone else's pain. Through a sincere apology, we create an opportunity for the person we have hurt to reconnect with us and find value in our relationship once again. A comprehensive apology, consisting of six layers, helps us to truly understand the extent of the harm we have caused.

Please refrain from using the six layers of an apology for your own control or outcome. If you do this, it will backfire and leave all involved with more disappointment. Apologies should not be used as a way to "one-up" or engage in a tit-for-tat situation. When an apology is manipulated, the individuals apologizing seek control out of fear but do not seek a sweet resolve.

The six layers of an apology done with venerability and from a secure heart comes from someone willing to absorb and feel another's pain. This is the kind of an apology that builds a solid bridge back to one another, one on which both parties can safely walk back and forth upon.

In the past, I would often say that I didn't want to make any mistakes because I didn't want to have to apologize. However, I have come to realize that when I cause harm, the six layers of apology, as suggested by the Miesners, helped me to find a positive and lasting resolution. Now, I actually enjoy apologizing. It feels gratifying to gain a deeper understanding of another individual by acknowledging their pain, even if the pain I caused was simply a result of reacting out of fear rather than acting with love and security.

The six layers of an apology looks like the following and in this exact order:

1. "I am sorry for what I've done."
2. "I take full responsibility for...(give details)."
3. "When I did this, it must have made you feel...(all about the other person in detail)."
4. "What can I do to make this right?"
5. "I've heard your pain so I am going to put a plan together to be sure this doesn't happen again."
6. "Will you please forgive me?" Be secure for any response they give. They may want to be mad at you a little longer. They may not want to trust you again until they see you've changed your behavior. However, when this is done with true, secure, honest intentions, the majority of people will accept this apology.

Understanding our emotions and empathizing with the feelings of others is crucial in resolving conflicts and tackling significant challenges. A genuine apology involves acknowledging and comprehending the emotions of the other person, as well as expressing regret for causing those emotions. By saying sorry, we demonstrate our awareness of the impact our actions have had on someone's feelings. Connecting with someone's pain holds a profound significance in facilitating collective healing.

Take the time to clearly communicate what you have done to the offended party. Remember that a reaction to an offense and the offense itself can stem from fear. Actions driven by fear usually require the six layers of an apology to initiate restoration. As we become more confident in loving both ourselves and others, we may apologize from a place of secure love, even if our apology is not accepted.

Breaking this down:

1. I am sorry for what I've done.

Are you genuinely remorseful for your actions, or are you solely regretful for being caught? If you truly intend to apologize, you must carefully examine this matter. Even if you haven't directly caused harm, you can still express regret for how your inaction or response may have affected someone's emotions.

This apology is not intended for minor incidents like accidentally spilling a drink from your hand. It is an apology for the distress caused by your behavior—a sincere acknowledgment of the wrongdoing you are aware of.

2. I take full responsibility for...

Deliberately speak your part of the offense. Maybe you laughed? Maybe that laugh was taken out of context and twisted for malicious gain, but still you laughed.

Maybe you need to take responsibility for knowing something was wrong, but you never said anything. You kept a secret or you kept silent. State it. Or perhaps you did something even more painful. Maybe you purposely did something you knew would be a massive betrayal and cruel. Say it.

3. When I did this, it must have made you feel...(all about the other person in detail)

This layer is important as it allows the other person to hear that you know what you did in detail to make them feel a specific way. You may even use the four communication goals to say, "You must have not felt safe, not felt in control, not felt liked, and or not felt right." Break it down. Write it down. Practice speaking this through. You want this to land in the center of the one person you offended.

4. What can I do to make this right?

Be quiet; listen. Come close. Pay attention. This could be a place of taking action to grow and learn. This can be a strategy to understand healthy, known, and kind expectations.

5. I've heard your pain, so I am going to put a plan together to be sure this doesn't happen again.

This is an ideal opportunity to emphasize the significance of layers one-to-four in your life. Perhaps counseling is something you would consider, indicating your willingness to take responsibility for your actions. Each situation will vary, yet by working together out of love for one another, you can find a resolution.

6. Will you please forgive me?

Be grateful for any response they provide. This aspect is highly sensitive. They may choose not to forgive you, and that is up to them, but you can forgive yourself. The consequences of a shattered trust may still exist, but you have taken the steps to restore it. You have initiated the process of repairing your side of the symbolic bridge.

You may never receive an apology, but you can offer one. A well-received apology has the power to diffuse a situation and make progress towards reaching a harmonious resolution. Your apology has the potential to completely transform a situation, or it may simply contribute to rekindling the positive feelings in your heart, knowing that you have done everything within your capability. Despite its difficulty, following the six layers of an apology allows you to apologize sincerely. As a result, you have successfully restored half of the figurative bridge between you and the other person.

Journal

1. List the six layers of an apology.
2. If you were offended, express the emotions it evoked and accept forgiveness.
3. Strive to forgive others, even in the absence of apologies.
4. As you progress towards a stronger self, you will be capable of both forgiving and apologizing. Mark this as proof of your growth.
5. If someone refuses to forgive you, practice self-forgiveness and grant them the necessary time and space.

Chapter 8

Forgiveness—Oh Yes, That...

Every day, estrangement rises and falls like the sun, as does the ongoing process of forgiveness. The process of forgiveness is a vital component of both reconciliation and restoration. Ongoing forgiveness can be one of the most challenging stages of forgiveness, as it requires forgiving someone who continues to repeat the action in need of forgiveness. Forgiveness is for all people; it has a price, and it is always worth it!

Forgiveness is for all people, really? Yes. In cases where forgiveness does not lead to restoration, we can acknowledge forgiveness as a concept. The person who chooses to forgive as a concept waits for time to bring about genuine feelings of forgiveness.

In the reality of estrangement, we are offered the option to choose forgiveness daily. Another day goes by without our daughter or mother. Another night is full of tossing and turning because we miss our daughter or mother. The pressures of regular and estranged life give us the option to forgive again and again. It's vital to choose the concept of forgiveness, as without it, our present and future looks grim. I don't want grim; I want gratefulness. It is excellent to say, "I agree with forgiveness; I'm not there yet, but I certainly forgive as a concept."

In the Christian environment, one may say, "I agree with the idea of forgiveness. I must rely on God's timing, justice, and mercy to change my heart regarding the offense. It's my job to agree with God for forgiveness, but it's God's job to transform my sorrow to joy." Forgiveness as a concept is a hard pill to swallow, especially the first time, but it is always the most freeing option. Practicing forgiveness halts the desire to react from a place of fear. Forgiveness in practice is a peaceful feeling even in the midst of an offense.

I have seen this powerful peace first hand demonstrated by a victim who instantly was forgiving during and after a brutal attack. It involved a 16-year-old teenager on roller skates who was skating in front of his house. Two boys known for bullying noticed him and approached him. They began to punch him.

Despite being repeatedly struck, I heard him say, "Jesus can forgive you for this too." Fortunately, the incident only lasted for a short while before the boys turned and walked away, laughing. Their laughter didn't sound like they were proud of their actions; rather, it had an underlying sense of shame. They had certainly sucker-punched him on roller skates. I never found out whether those boys ever apologized to him or not.

Witnessing this event highlighted how difficult it is to offer forgiveness, especially when it isn't acknowledged or received at the moment of offense. The 16-year-old receiving the abuse eventually grew up to lead a significant ministry in his community. On that day, when he was attacked, he truly understood the power of forgiveness; he had already resolved within himself to align with complete forgiveness as a teenager, and in the moment! As he spoke to his attackers, I could sense his agreement with forgiveness because he knew that someone greater than himself was responsible for the true work of forgiveness: Jesus Christ.

It is crucial to acknowledge that not all Christians exhibit such exemplary behavior. Just ask my children about my reactive moments before forgiveness overcame me. We are all imperfect beings who continuously learn and grow throughout our journey, including myself. I am aware of my flaws and how easily I may say something inappropriate in a moment of reaction. However, I strongly believe in the power of forgiveness, both towards others and oneself. While it may seem painfully contradictory at times, embracing forgiveness allows it to blossom within us.

Forgiveness is costly, particularly when something or someone dear to us has been hurt or offended. It's relatively easy to forgive minor incidents such as forgetting to return an item, but forgiving painful deep relationship issues is an entirely different matter. It is hard and it costs!

When we start seeing forgiveness as a personal choice that is more costly to withhold, over time we will experience its liberating power. When we forgive someone, we release ourselves from the burden of holding them in contempt.

Although we are not judges in a courtroom, refusing to forgive can make us feel entitled to condemn.

The medical profession sees forgiveness as good medicine as demonstrated in articles like *Forgiveness in Health Research and Medical Practice* by Worthington, Witvliet, Lerner, and Scherer.

Forgiveness (Worthington, 2005) has been ingrained in humanity for centuries, and all religions recognize it as a deeply rooted aspect that is divine. The power of forgiveness knows no bounds and can penetrate deeply into our lives.

Worthington, in his 2005 article, stated that when a government is unable to forgive, it resembles a warring entity, hindering progress and unity. In our quest to maintain mental well-being, forgiveness emerges as an essential area deserving of attention. It's important to note that forgiveness does not automatically equate to reconciliation. Merely dwelling on offenses instead of accepting the need for forgiveness repeatedly can have detrimental effects on our sleep, daily lives, and even digestion. In conclusion, this article emphasized the significance of promoting forgiveness alongside justice because forgiving others holds tremendous importance, regardless of the way it is expressed by individuals.

When forgiveness goes beyond being just a theoretical concept to agree with, a new hope emerges within the mind. As we clear the way for new thoughts, we create new experiences focusing on something we really love and enjoy. This part is the divine mystery.

Forgiveness fully realized does have restoration, but it costs someone something. It's an enigma when we forgive with no reconciliation because we can't quite figure out how we got there. Just by agreeing with the concept of forgiveness, suddenly we are not triggered as easily. Where we were once stuck on past offenses, only new experiences exist. Enjoying new experiences is possible with forgiveness as a concept even without reconciliation.

Recently, while grocery shopping, two little kids were in a grocery cart. Their sister, who was maybe a year older, was walking beside them with one hand on the grocery cart. The mom was focused on shopping, but the little sister was looking back with a plotting look of revenge toward her siblings sitting there in the cart seats. The cart seats had steering wheels. She must have wanted to be the one riding and driving. I giggled to myself noticing what was happening. I couldn't help thinking of how adults act the same way. How often do we reject forgiveness, wearing a frowning face and plotting revenge as a way of getting even?

Everyone needs to learn to forgive and practice forgiving from childhood through our golden years. I was truly taken aback when I came across Ruth Graham's book, "Forgiving My Father, Forgiving Myself." It seemed incomprehensible to me that she would have anything negative to say about her father, Billy Graham. Upon seeing the title, I couldn't help but wonder what Billy Graham could have possibly done to cause harm to one of his children. Growing up in church and admiring figures like Billy Graham, it seemed as though they were the epitome of a loving and devoted family, the kind every girl in Sunday school hoped her father would be like, and perhaps even marry.

However, in 2019 while sitting in a coffee shop, I spent hours engrossed in Ruth's entire book. I absorbed every word as if my life depended on it. It was then that I realized Ruth had experienced a good childhood with some big let downs. Despite this reality, she held onto resentment towards a father who was wholeheartedly serving his ministry calling, even if it meant a lot of time away from home. This revelation shocked me.

Deep down inside her heart, Ruth still missed her dad dearly. His constant travels prevented him from being fully present for her and this absence constituted its own form of trauma for which she had no control or say over. Acknowledging, repenting, and forgiving were necessary even for the tiniest disappointments on the spectrum of letdowns, including with a father like Billy Graham. To know forgiveness, one has to agree with it first. Then by embracing agreement, the process of forgiving every dit-dot of even the tiniest letdown to the worst happens.

Incomplete agreement of forgiveness is similar to a persistent weed root that keeps growing, even when its top is cut off. This can be quite annoying, much like an irritating weed. The overwhelming desire for justice often drowns out any mercy. However, mercy without justice is fragile, like building a house with straw that easily blows away in the first wind storm. Forgiveness flourishes when there is a delicate balance of justice and mercy, leading us toward peace. Attaining this balance seems difficult or unachievable in our imperfect world where justice is often scarce.

Forgiveness becomes even more difficult when it is not accompanied by a balance of mercy and justice. Although we have the capacity to show mercy, when it seems like the wrongdoer continuously avoids any form of accountability, it makes forgiveness seem like an abstract concept for all time.

Have you ever come across well-meaning individuals who urge you to forgive without acknowledging that forgiveness entails certain sacrifices? It demands both mercy and justice. Without these elements, peace cannot be attained. Therefore, how do we discover the strength to forgive completely in such circumstances? How can we forgive when there is no justice present? However, if there is too much justice and no mercy, life is over and forgiveness never has a chance.

The real question is, can we give forgiveness a chance? Can we release the pain caused by someone's actions or lack thereof? Can we temporarily detach the offense from our own humanity and embrace forgiveness?

In the 1976 book, "The Sunflower" by Simon Wiesenthal, a prominent figure in the fight for justice for Jewish holocaust victims, wrote his main theme about the ability to give forgiveness. The book recounts Wiesenthal's experience as a Jewish prisoner during the Holocaust, where he was confronted with a dying Nazi who sought his forgiveness for his role in killing Jews. However, Wiesenthal chose not to grant this forgiveness.

The latter half of the book delves into the question of whether one could forgive a Nazi for committing such heinous war crimes. Many people in the book give reasons to forgive or not. For those who grapple with forgiving others, the section provides insight into the challenges posed by forgiveness. While acknowledging that the Nazi's actions were both atrocious and driven by unjust government orders, even those who believed in and practiced forgiveness struggled to extend it to the dying Nazi.

As I read the responses of other Jews when asked if they would have forgiven, I noticed that the real issue was just deciding to forgive. Somehow in each case, forgiveness was an option in their own hands to choose. Forgiveness is in our hands now, we just have to decide to forgive.

In our human nature, we may verbally agree to the idea of forgiveness even before justice or mercy is received. While the concept of forgiveness is agreeable, actually practicing and embodying it feels impossible. Just when we believe we have moved on from a situation, it can unexpectedly resurface due to various triggers like an event, a movie, a photo shared on social media, or in a news article.

If genuine forgiveness requires a blend of justice and mercy, how does this harmonious combination come to be when, like an obnoxious weed, the grudge-filled soul sprouts up to remind us we have a choice again and again? I do believe the mystery lies within us to choose forgiveness: to cut that grudge off at the root. When triggers poke us, or a careless person reminds us our forgiveness isn't complete, remember that their own blindness cannot see the forgiveness we have agreed with because they are looking for complete reconciliation. When this happens, go back to the oral agreement to forgive. Know somewhere there will be a cost for the offense to be weighed and measured with justice; for now, give yourself the mercy to wait upon the mystery of forgiveness.

Time is on your side when you order up forgiveness in the face of triggers and careless words thrusted your way. Even those careless words said to you about your lack of forgiveness will be weighed and measured somewhere in the future according to Jesus himself. Jesus said in Matt. 12:36, *"I tell you, son the day of judgment people will give account for every careless word they speak."*

To illustrate the concept of forgiveness without reconciliation, let's imagine ordering a cocktail. First we order it, and then we anticipate its arrival. The bartender must meticulously prepare it before serving it to us. While this analogy may seem trivial, for individuals witnessing forgiveness in action, imagine Jesus as the bartender. A forgiving drink consists of two ingredients: justice and mercy. The ring of the glass is a mix of sweet and sour because it is sweet to receive forgiveness and bitter to give it. Jesus mixes them together for us to partake. Our part was ordering it; the part of the drink being completed belongs to the bartender.

Who pays the ultimate cost for this cocktail we have ordered up? Jesus. The mercy was the sweet part demonstrating love for our deepest pain in death. The crucifixion was justice. Jesus was willing to be crucified for all times, for all people, and for the smallest offense to the worst. He paid the debt of death once and for all for those who would believe in Him, John 1:12.

Jesus knows how hard it is for us to forgive. He sweated blood at the thought of how gruesome and painful forgiveness would cost! *Luke 22:44, "And being in agony he prayed more earnestly;*

and his sweat became like great drops of blood falling down to the ground." Somehow this was the cost of justice, paying a price for every wrong over all time. At the cross where Jesus was, is where we lay our offering of the forgiveness concept.

The cross is where we exchange our trespasses for hope. When we, like Jesus, embrace forgiveness through the cross, we too agree that we believe we will be resurrected and ascend to Heaven, where all tears are wiped away (Revelation 21:4). Jesus gave all of his perfect self through the act of the crucifixion, the resurrection, and the ascension. He alone is the bartender of the drink called forgiveness.

Our first part is to decide to enter into the agreement of forgiveness. Each step is difficult as memories of what we are forgiving obstruct our path. Walking towards forgiveness is a challenging task. Somehow, we finally sit and look deep into what it costs us if we do not forgive. What has been done has been done. Do we continue to add thoughts, words, and actions that will be weighed and measured for justice and mercy?

Secondly, when we agree with forgiveness it demonstrates our readiness and longing for forgiveness for ourselves from our own offenses. Somehow, time and endurance gives into a fuller forgiveness. When we realize Jesus came to Earth for us, the Holy Ghost penetrates and floods us with forgiveness deeply.

If you are not familiar with Jesus Christ and his teachings from the Bible, you can learn about his life by studying the four books of the New Testament: Matthew, Mark, Luke, and John. The Bible GateWay app provides free access to various versions of the Bible. Some of my personal favorites include the Mounce Reverse Interlinear New Testament, which translates Greek to English; EVS, a version I used for this book; and The Message, which has a narrative style similar to a movie script.

In our modern era, we often lack a true understanding of how a crucifixion would appear. By examining certain verses, we can deduce that even the cloth depicted on Jesus in various artworks was likely not an accurate representation, but rather a symbol of our own spiritual shelter. Jesus willingly bore the weight of every sin ever committed, from the very first transgression to the final ones, even for the ones we hold grudges for in estrangement. How bad was paying the cost for our own transgressions?

Isaiah in the Old Testament wrote that the one who would give us salvation would be mutilated beyond recognition. Isaiah 15:14, *"As many were astonished at you- his appearance was so marred, beyond human semblance, and his form beyond that of the children of mankind..." Is. 50:6 , "I gave my back to those who strike, and my cheeks to those who pull out the beard; I hid not my face from disgrace and spitting."* Sounds like a crucifixion.

The New Testament told what happened in Jesus' time on Earth. *Matt. 26:67, "Then they spit in his face and struck him. And some slapped him,..." Luke 22:64, "They also blindfolded him and kept asking him, "Prophesy! Who is it that struck you?" Mark 15:19, "And they were striking his head with a reed and spitting on him and kneeling down in homage to him." Luke 22:63, "Now the men who were holding Jesus in custody were mocking him as they beat him." John 19:33-34, "But when they came to Jesus and saw that he was already dead, they did not break his legs. But one of the soldiers pierced his side with a spear, and at once there came out blood and water."*

This is quite gruesome especially if one has never come across these Scriptures or viewed Jesus as anything other than a teacher or a historical figure from the past. However, upon examining what was prophesied about him and what actually transpired, it becomes clear that if he allowed those events to unfold, he possessed a profound comprehension of justice and mercy equalizing forgiveness for the offender and the victim. Jesus implored his Heavenly father for an alternative course of action if one existed. There was none; forgiveness necessitated the payment of justice which could not be evaded. If anyone possesses the answer to forgiveness, it is Jesus himself in the life he lived here on Earth.

We are definitely not Jesus, but many of us have felt like we have been crushed, whipped, struck, and spit on with words or real spit. We have been deceived. We have all been wronged. You name it, it happened to Jesus. He can relate to us. We can relate to him.

Somewhere, forgiveness is worth dying for. Somehow, it will cost us all. It will never cost us what it cost God the Father sending his Son, Jesus. It will never cost us what it cost Jesus. Somehow, somewhere, right now our grudges can disappear like death that loosened its hold on Jesus. We can rise up out of the unforgiven grudge life. We can experience the freedom of something new by agreeing with the concept of forgiveness.

Based on the Christian concept, when one immerses oneself in the memory of Jesus Christ's crucifixion, it becomes evident that the only offenses on Jesus are those that we have offered to him to take from us. When we agree with forgiveness; somehow those offenses are placed in Jesus' hands, and we are free. This freedom gives us peace. This peace is a person: Jesus.

We may never be able to resolve the intricacies of repairing something that we and others have destroyed, nor can we change the past. However, we can embrace the concept of forgiveness because it gives us peace, and Jesus somehow works out the rest. How wonderful it would be to come back home, completely forgiven.

*****Journal*

1. Write down what you want forgiveness for.
2. Write what has happened to you.
3. Agree that God will help you forgive.
4. Agree that God will give you his understanding of forgiveness.
5. Agree with the concept of forgiveness.

Chapter 9

Bridge Builders or Bomb Builders: It Is up to Us; Which Are We?

Throughout this chapter, I'd like to use the symbolism of building a bridge where each brick is unbreakable and placed securely in its rightful place. The bridge then gives strength and security for all who cross. Examining a good thing as if it is a symbolic brick for building a bridge or a symbolic brick for bombing a bridge helps us see how we can all choose to build or destroy our own security with ourselves and others.

Somehow, both bridge and bomb builders have learned their respective crafts through life experiences. It is easy to be a bomb builder, but it requires skill and a willingness to try, especially from a place of pain, to be a bridge builder. Safeguarding our words and thoughts is an essential part of becoming a master bridge builder.

When it comes to an estrangement, if we want to repair, each person must build their side of a bridge. All the bricks on one side must support that side alone. The other side can only be built on the opposite side of land. Think this: This side, that side, my side, your side. Get it?

Picture a bombed side of a bridge: people can walk on the side still remaining. Now imagine each side bombed. What happens? That bridge is no more.

Consider the bomb builders of relationships, when they toss a bomb they are weakening their own side because they had to use one of their own bricks to build that bomb! Likewise, if the bridge builder has all their bricks securely intact and in their rightful place, that side is secure. The lobbed brick bomb may hit the bridge builder's side, but it will not break it.

When it comes to building our personal bridge for others to walk across, any time we take a good or valuable thing and turn it into something ultimate, it becomes a vice. Soon it will decisively begin to tick away like a bomb. It starts ticking because it was never made to take the pressure of being someone's ultimate thing. Soon, the holder of this ultimate brick will become a manipulator, an accuser, a deceiver, and a prideful envious bomb builder. All of us, even if we are not aware, are capable of blowing up our own side of our bridge.

The good news is that we bomb builders—including me—can purposely transform to become a skilled bridge builder. Mothers and daughters alike are capable of both roles. Choosing and remaining to work in the guild of bridge builders requires courage and honesty. Just admitting that in the past we tossed brick bombs from our ultimate good brick weaponry, is one step closer to taking that ultimate brick and putting it back in its rightful place, for good. Its place is on its own secure side of our bridge for us and for others to rely on when needed.

Ultimate good brick bombs will blow up when we least expect it. As a middle schooler, I learned that two older high school boys thought it would be a great idea to make a liquid bomb to toss on a metal mascot at a rival high school. The boys plotted and toiled. In the car with the bomb liquid in hand, while driving to their target, the liquid blew up in one of the boy's hands! He lost a few fingers, but each gained a new insight into how bombs could go off even when one doesn't expect it. These boys had taken the good brick of sportsmanship for school rivalry to an ultimate thing sparking their prideful envy to get one up on the other school. The other school's mascot remains today. The boy's fingers? Still gone.

Good things become bad things when they are used for complete security in some areas of our lives. We all want security, but latching onto something good can soon become a false security. For example, if we joined a business Zoom meeting with a blanket and a pacifier, we would be laughed at because everyone knows a pacifier and a baby blanket are only good in their own place: with a baby. When we lose a good thing that we thought was an ultimate thing, we lose the security it gave us.

Knowing that we are secure, regardless of a challenge we face, is a good sign that our "emotional security" is in line with a bridge builder instead of a bomb builder.[4] When we have taken something positive and made it the ultimate focus in our

---

[4] Warren, 2024 ^

life, our emotional balance may be lacking. When the ultimate thing is no longer ours to manipulate and control, soothing our own personal fears becomes impossible—so we think. On December 26, 2017, Tim Keller Wisdom tweeted: "Sin isn't just about doing bad things; it's more about turning good things into ultimate things."

The concept of portraying one's emotional security centering on a good thing as an ultimate thing is portrayed in C.S. Lewis's play "The Great Divorce" published in 1945. Lewis's characters are depicted as living for a good thing. They each have one chance to let go of that good thing, or go to Hell. In order to progress into Heaven, they must let go of this misplaced priority and refocus on what truly matters: God's love. In this story, what matters is what is on the other side of letting go of the good thing one made ultimate: Heaven.

In "The Great Divorce," what resonated with me was the portrayal of the self-loving mother who had made her role as a mom her ultimate focus. Boom! That was my own personal bomb, making the role of a mom an ultimate thing. I'd made my love of my children an idol-brick of emotional security. That brick was brutal; I had positioned it out of place. The pain of forgiving myself was almost unbearable. Being a mom is a good thing, but being a mom also means letting our kids find their own way and trusting them. This metaphorical bomb took me from doing good things as a mom, to doing ultimate things. When those ultimate things did not go my way, it weakened my side of my bridge, not only as a mom but in my perception of myself as a loved child of God Himself.

I've met a lot of self-loving mothers, but I had blinders on when I acted like one. Long before my estrangement from my

114

children, I'd often wonder why moms especially would purposely "blow up" a relationship with their children. I could see it happening in them. I remember thinking I never wanted to be that way, but as my estrangement loomed, my own self-loving mother vice self-slipped in like an invisible person causing fear, stress, and frustration for everyone.

When we act like bomb builders, we will do anything if we don't get what we want. At the core of fear-driven emotions, the hardening of our hearts can take on the power of a runaway train, full steam ahead. When we are like this, we are not only being a bomb builder who will be surprised when the bomb blows up in our face, but we cannot stop ourselves any more than a runaway train can stop itself.

When self-love overruns the good of a relationship between a mom and a daughter, it is never due to one factor. On top of an ultimate good thing will be stacked many little problematic things. Many of the self-loving mothers I had known previously confided in me that their marriages were already deteriorating at the time their words were so heavy upon their own daughters. They told me they felt they couldn't confide in anyone at that time. Consequently, these moms found themselves leaning heavily on their relationships with their daughters as an outlet or security for the mounting pressure within their marriages. I did too.

When I first experienced estrangement from my own children, I was bewildered and shocked. My body felt numb, and it was difficult to feel anything at all. A few days later I stopped at a restaurant, where an older woman happened to be sitting next to me. I spoke with her about the recent estrangement with my children, and the deep sorrow it had caused me. Her response scared me! She showed me the potential outcome if I wasn't willing to seek real security.

In that moment, it became clear to me that this woman lacked something very important: the honor and respect of her own son. As a result, she carried a heavy emotional burden that she weaponized, and it slashed at me. Reflecting on this encounter afterwards, I realized how fortunate I was to witness her reaction so early on in my own experience of estrangement. It reminded me of why becoming bitter or resorting to hurtful words against my children would not solve anything, but could make it worse—way worse!

This woman taught me a valuable lesson: symbolically building bombs is never the answer when faced with problems within family relationships. Even if everything seems to be falling apart in a family, be a bridge builder—especially if you are the only one left standing.

Mrs. Bomb Builder mentioned that her son had stopped talking to her after she and his father had given him a substantial amount of money for his business. When his father had had a heart attack and was in the hospital, the son had chosen to watch football with his friends instead of being by his father's side. His father had died before he could make it to the hospital. I remember commenting, "You must have really trusted your son to give him such a large amount of money. Perhaps you can find it in your heart to forgive him?"

She adamantly refused. Her face turned furiously red and she quickly gulped down her cocktail as if trying to numb her pain or calm herself. The veins on her neck bulged so aggressively that I hoped she would not pass out! Bitterness was evident.

She declared that even if she saw her son after death, she would spit in his face. I thought to myself, "Please God, don't let me succumb to such negative thoughts." I shared her pain, but I did not want to share anything else with her. I saw how damaging pain could be if I were to let my own pain blind me.

I'm sure she never planned to be where she was, and I know I did not plan where I was. She showed me that I did not want to take one step closer to whatever it was that had landed both her and me estranged. I was determined to recover and rebuild, even if I had no idea at that time how to do it.

A year after my own children became estranged I also witnessed a daughter who had an inflated condemning attitude bomb ticking so loud that everyone was looking at her. I was strolling down the street in NYC when I noticed a young woman, approximately 27 years old, walking alongside her friend. She complained to her friend, "I can't stand my mother! She expects me to text her that I received $5,000 for my rent. What a terrible person she is! It's as if she's doing me some kind of favor by letting me live here! I truly despise her." This young woman was so consumed by her pride as her ultimate thing that she failed to notice the grief and disgust on her friend's face. From what I could gather, it looked like the shocked friend paid for her own rent. The surprised friend likely had multiple roommates or even someone renting out her couch to cover her rent. She would have loved to have someone pay her $5,000 rental fee to live in her own personal apartment. All the daughter needed to do was send a short text to her mom expressing gratitude for providing the rent money. However, gratitude appeared to be disregarded in favor of whatever mattered most to this daughter.

The two, the mother at the bar and the daughter walking the sidewalk reminded me of the Bible story of the Pharaoh of Egypt in the book of Exodus. Pharaoh had it all, and still he was a hardened bomb builder. When Moses approached Pharaoh and requested the liberation of the Hebrew people from slavery, an intriguing pattern emerged. Each time one of the plagues occurred, the Pharaoh's heart would become hardened, or more accurately, strengthened to go against the God of Moses. It was as if Pharaoh fortified himself against Moses like a determined boxer in a ring. In Hebrew, "harden" implies strengthening or toughening up. It looks like this from the Accordance Bible software:

harden חָזַק A Verb -sounds like "piel" - perfect first common singular consecutive to be strong. חִזַּקְתִּי

Notice Pharaoh, despite being human, managed to gather strength and lead his troops into battle after seven plagues, including the last which took his son's life! To him, lording over the Hebrews was his right because his kingship was the ultimate thing, even over God Himself. He fought relentlessly to maintain his control over the people who he considered his slaves. His heart was hard!

If you have ever delved into the study of ancient Egyptian pharaohs, you would know that their belief in multiple gods was commonplace. These Pharaohs believed they were god-like beings themselves. In Pharaoh's eyes, he was the epitome of power and authority: His way was deemed supreme. However, this so-called "ultimate" power proved to be fleeting, as Pharaoh not only lost his grip on the enslaved Hebrews, his hardened heart led him to his own demise.

As estranged moms and daughters, we should consider what good thing was so important to us that it led to this estrangement. What we thought was so significant, was not as significant as we thought. As life has gone on, I've learned to practice putting my ultimate things back in their rightful good place.

When we are burdened by the actions of being a bomb builder, it may feel like a new beginning is unimaginable. However, others who've come before us have discovered inner peace. We too can achieve tranquility by releasing our unhealthy attachments. We can endure any challenges as long as we prioritize positive aspects in our lives and guard our own thoughts to cling onto false security. The answer lies in embracing a life without full reliance on even important relationships.

I know this to be true because even in the midst of the pain of estrangement, once-hidden abilities within myself are now blooming because I no longer rely on my ultimate relationships before estrangement. Being cut off from my loved ones forced me to nurture my own creativity. Writing a book was never something I had considered. I never imagined I'd write a book designed to help women in similar situations to forge forward and empower friendships with others who share the same fate.

Estrangement unexpectedly led me down this path to discover my forgotten inner strength and desire, not only for my own talents, but also for fellowship with other women. It became necessary for me to persevere and rise above the overwhelming sadness caused by broken relationships. At the end of a war, what do the people do? They rebuild.

I have encountered numerous older women who have also achieved a sense of tranquility with regard to their estranged child or mother. They have been a source of security and safety for me and others. I've come across these remarkable individuals within Church communities. Their determination stems from the knowledge that they remain at peace even with the ebb and flow of lament, despite having no knowledge about their child or mother.

Initially, their serenity provided me comfort, but now it fills me with hope, fortitude, and courage. They have successfully constructed their side of the bridge and I am familiar with it. In fact, I have traversed these bridges myself and can attest to their solidity, security, and reliability. They've shown me that no one is more capable than fighting for our own peaceful resolution than ourselves.

When I first met these women, I thought "What in the world? Who could do something so cruel to these women?" They would speak of issues that were in and out of their control, dividing them from their loved ones. They would talk of reaching out, with no avail. They often would say things like "I'm used to it. My children don't speak to me after our divorce." Or, "I can't do anything about it. So now I work on self-care and make the most of every day." I've also heard, "I've given my daughter over to the Lord. If she doesn't want to come and see me after 40 years, then I need to respect that and know God loves her more than I do. For whatever reason this is the path she chose. She has never let me offer restoration on my side. One can forgive, but it takes two to restore what each of us dismantled."

In my personal being when I have all good things in their rightful place, I strongly believe everyone must find their unique path which can often be filled with potholes, pivots, and boulders. This is figuratively of course but even figurative emotions can crush our heart. Remember Jesus? Did you know before he asked his Father in Heaven if there was another way, He actually fell on his face and said, "My soul is very sorrowful, even to death; remain here, and watch with me." [5]

If Jesus was crushed with a heart of agony walking his own unique path, should we be so shocked to discover that we too will experience the crushing in our hearts for the sorrow we endure? Fortunately, we are not being crucified, but the first church for 360 years was fed to lions and worse. Like Jesus, they willingly walked their unique path as their security was in God, not on an ultimate thing.

Unfortunately, everyone's path on this love train called Earth will be paved with crushing agony at times, but we can endure. I promise. Endurance is something humans are very good at, especially when we are secure in our own identity and our own faith in the evidence of the good to come. [6] Estranged people who use this time to grow, long for the day of resolve. That is a good hope to look forward to.

Since 2011 when my mother became estranged from me, and then my children in 2018, my endurance resolve is now lioness-like. I have intentionally taken actions to heal myself

---

[5] Matt. 26:38

[6] Hebrews 11:1-6

and strive towards becoming a safer individual for anyone who enters my life. Much like the other ladies who've done this before me, somehow when the flow of agony visits me, it always fades like a fever which eventually breaks.

It is my intention not to cause any further harm to those around me, while also recognizing the importance of forgiving the pain others have caused me. Sometimes when it comes to how others have caused us pain, we think that what they did was worse than anything. Soon, we alone are their judge, jury, and executioner. I'm sorry, but a bridge builder leaves that thought dormant.

As a chosen bridge builder, I am determined to distance myself from any conflicts or confrontations where bomb builders dwell. This does not mean I will shut people out of my life. Instead, I will purposely come near to let them know they are invited to the bridge builders' guild. Yet, I will not linger in the bomb builders guild with them. I don't belong there. Nor do you. Sometimes this works; sometimes it doesn't, but at least we can try to demonstrate a builders mindset. It is ultimately our choice of what we want to be: a bridge builder or a bomb builder.

Journal thoughts of a bridge builder:

1. Always remember that our Creator has the ability to open doors that no human being can close. Pray that God will open a door to this estrangement that can never be shut again (Isaiah 22:22, Revelation 3:7-8, Ephesians 3:20, Matthew 19:26).

2. Practice patience and wait upon Him. What are you currently waiting for? (Isaiah 40:31, Lamentations 3:25, Psalm 33:20-22).
3. Take moments of stillness and embrace tranquility in your solitude (Proverbs 3:24, Psalm 131:2).
4. Engage in meditation to fill yourself with focusing on what is virtuous, true, righteous, kind, and loving.
5. Pay attention to your thoughts and evaluate them in order to build yourself up and provide encouragement.
6. Bridge builder's Proverb bricks: Proverbs 15:14, Proverbs 10:12, Proverbs 17:17, Proverbs 29:11, Proverbs 15:18.
7. We are advised not to seek revenge, but to trust in the Lord for deliverance from evil intentions. Proverbs 20:22.

Chapter 10

The Expectant Woman: Expectancy and Our Inheritance of the Holy Spirit

Jeremiah 31:33, "I will put my law within them, and I will write it on their hearts. And I will be their God, and they shall be my people."

The book of Jeremiah was written over 600 years before Christ. This verse promised an expectant hope for those who wanted God inside of their own hearts. Like Jeremiah who looked forward to receiving God within, all who have Jesus have the Holy Spirit within. God will not estrange himself from us, because the Holy Spirit proceeds from God and comes to

ESTRANGEMENT; HEALING FOR MOTHERS AND DAUGHTERS

us through Jesus. The Holy Spirit is our seal, protection, and inheritance that God put in our hearts as foretold from Jeremiah 31:33.

In my sealed heart, joy sings like a morning bird, announcing the sun rising despite the turbulent nights before. This hope illuminates, like the moon piercing the darkness of fallacy, pain, and deception. During the early stages of my childhood faith, this hope felt as small as a dime in my chest. Now it has grown so large that it encompasses most of my being. This sealed joy that is protected as my inheritance because of Jesus remains steadfast in spite of my failings.

If Jesus inherits us with all our failings, we too inherit Him with all his goodness. An equally good part we inherit from Jesus is the Holy Spirit proceeding from Him to us. Have you noticed in scripture how the Holy Spirit is connected to Jesus? He goes where Jesus is or has been.

As mothers, is there any place our daughters have gone that we would not explore after them? When I reflected on the reality that the Holy Spirit came after Jesus in the book of Acts, I began to intentionally acknowledge this Holy Spirit movement.

Now, when I catch myself saying "Jesus," I purposely give a nod or a word to the Holy Spirit. This acknowledgement discipline has transformed much of my human weakness into endurance and self-control. I cannot tell you how this happens; only that it has.

In 2018, a few months after I began this discipline, Jesus came to me in a dream. A week afterward, a Jewish believer said, "Jodi, I was startled in my dream last night. Jesus came to me and he showed me your dream." He then went on to explain my dream in full detail.

I tried to trick him and I said, "Was I in my living room or kitchen?" He said, "No Jodi, you were sitting on your side of bed and then Jesus stood you up. You thought you were done here. Jesus said, "Go back and keep doing what you are doing."

I did see Jesus coming towards me while I was in my bed fast asleep. I sat up. Then he stood me up! His hands came towards me first. They had holes in them the size of a pop can. I looked into those holes that were black and deep like an abyss. I felt the deepest sorrow knowing those holes were somehow my doing. His glorious face beamed with love and acceptance. He stood me up from my bed and held me close. His long, square chin sat upon my head and his hands held my back under my shoulder blades. I could see a big blue light between our chests that was connected to him. It appeared to be the size of a basketball. It was also remarkably huge. As I looked into the blue light, I wondered if the golden flecks in that light were all of us who love Him. There was a massive sound, much like the sound of a plane taking off, but louder. He took me far above Earth and as I looked down, I said, "Well, this is it. I cannot help my children or husband anymore." Then in an instant, I was awake, standing next to my bed with my head down. My long shag carpet was squeezed between my toes.

Before this dream and before my estrangement from my daughter and son, I kept having heart pain and dreaming I was going to pass out. I knew somehow something was coming. Once my estrangement actually happened and the only joy within was from the Holy Spirit, the dream of Jesus coming to me was a dream putting all the bad dreams in their place. No matter what would happen, God the Father, Jesus the Son, and the Holy Spirit had me fully secure.

I didn't know then, but now I know, as the Holy Spirit grieved within me over what was going on that I could not see, He was also awakening me to my own creativity in learning to listen to him more. Cultivating my creativity to write this book is a part of sharing my testimony for others, but it was born from the Holy Spirit sealing me, protecting me, and giving to me abundantly of my heavenly inheritance.

The Holy Spirit did not just come after Jesus in the book of Acts, He also indwells inside of us as we yield to Jesus. Have you noticed when we focus on what God says about those he loves, (us) dread fades? Joy and hope abound, almost instantly much deeper than the pain. This is some kind of a divine attribute from the Holy Spirit making God's law of love settle deep within our hearts.

The gifts and fruits of the Holy Spirit are our inheritance to reap and share also. This allows the Holy Spirit within us to grow so big, we pour out these gifts and fruits for others to also enjoy. Before estrangement, my self-control fruit was a pomegranate seed. Now my self-control fruit has grown to the size of a blue-ribbon, award-winning giant pumpkin found at a country fair. I did not expect my fruit of self-control to grow so much, but God did.

The whole Bible uses fruits as an allegory. The first fruit that has meaning is in Gen. 3 when Adam and Eve ate it. That one fruit, led to death. The Holy Ghost gives us eight fruits! These fruits give us life abundantly to feast upon and share with others. *Gal. 5:22–23: "Love, peace, patience, kindness, goodness, faithfulness, gentleness and self-control."*

The Holy Spirit was known by John the Baptist who literally only ate honey and grasshoppers.[7] John was expectant of two things: Jesus and the Holy Spirit.[8] From what is recorded about John the Baptist, we know he was expecting some kind of restoration from that bitter-sweet fruit Adam and Eve ate! Did he know the Holy Ghost would give us such incredible spiritual fruit?

The Holy Spirit would be a helper, a witness, a comforter and more. [9] When Jesus ascended into Heaven from the Earth, all of the disciples and believers had an expectant heart waiting for the Holy Spirit. Ten days later at Pentecost when travelers far and wide came to the holiday, the Holy Spirit came upon all who trusted Jesus! Acts 2:1–31 recalls how many were amazed at the presence of the Holy Spirit. Those who had a hopeful heart, remembering Jesus had promised that the Holy Spirit would come, joyfully experienced the abundant outpouring of the Holy Spirit during the Pentecost in the book of Acts.

The Holy Spirit was expected to arrive because Jesus said He would. As we journey along with the Holy Spirit indwelling within us, God the Father's will is completed or sealed in his workmanship: us. Our inheritance in the Heavenly realms and

---

[7] Matt. 3:4

[8] Mark 1:7–8

[9] John 15

within us now, stands secure even in an estrangement. Expect it!

No one can rip Jesus or our inheritance from God's own hand. Not even estrangement! *Isaiah 41:10, "Fear not for I am with you; be not dismayed, for I am your God; I will strengthen you, I will help you, I will uphold you with my righteous right hand." John 10:28–30*, Jesus said, *"I give them eternal life, and they will never perish, and no one will snatch them out of my hand. My Father, who has given them to me, is greater than all, and no one is able to snatch them out of the Father's hand. I and the Father are one."*

When James, the brother of Jesus, reminds us the Holy Ghost will complete our inheritance, he means it! The Holy Spirit will not withhold anything back from us. [ESVS] *James 1:4, "And let steadfastness have its full effect, that you may be perfect and complete, lacking in nothing."* Estrangement definitely teaches us to be steadfast or unwavering in our love for our mother and daughters.

The mother-daughter relationship portrays a natural inheritance, but with God we have a supernatural inheritance. *Eph. 1:13–14, "In him you also, when you heard the word of truth, the gospel of your salvation, and believed in him, were sealed with the promised Holy Spirit, who is the guarantee of our inheritance until we acquire possession of it, to the praise of his glory."*

Phil. 1:6 reminds us, " ... that he who began a good work in you will bring it to completion at the day of Jesus Christ." Isn't becoming a mother a good work that God began when he gave us our mother/daughter relationship! Keep this verse close to you too, and expect God to complete his good work for yourself, your daughter and your mother. If somehow the good work of God is complete in us, so too does he care about the good work and inheritances of our mothers and daughters being complete in them.

We have no idea how grand our inheritance with God is; 1 Cor. 2:9 says, " *But, as it is written, "What no eye has seen, nor ear heard, nor the heart of man imagined, what God has prepared for those who love him."*

Our inheritance includes the Holy Spirit's wisdom that helps us to be kind, to forgive, to put away our bomb-builder mindset. *James 1:5 says, "If any of you lacks wisdom, let him ask God, who gives generously to all without reproach, and it will be given him."*

We may choose to trust God's plan over the details within our mother-daughter estrangement. *Prov. 3:5, "Trust in the LORD with all your heart, and do not lean on your own understanding."*

We may believe that our pain is evidence of God disowning us from the inheritance we hope for, which we cannot yet see. However, Scripture reminds us that there is much more beyond what we can currently perceive. In both the present and the future, God will not deprive us of any good thing.[10]

Each time we experience the wave of heartache, understand that it is an opportunity for courage to grow inside of our spiritual fruits. As we practice cultivating an attitude of

---

[10] Psalms 84:11

expectancy, we are helping ourselves to quickly regain mental balance and emotional intelligence that will allow us to one day fully realize how the bad will be turned for good. Remember Joseph in Gen. 50:20 when he forgave his brothers for beating him and selling him as a slave? He said, *"As for you, you meant evil against me, but God meant it for good, to bring it about that many people should be kept alive, as they are today."*

For me, years of estrangement lie behind and perhaps await me in the future. However, I maintain a consistent routine before I drift off to sleep. I engage in the practice of praying Scripture over myself. Nothing alleviates the pain quite like reciting a verse from the Scriptures. With the anticipation that comes from embracing God's word, I firmly believe that I have an inheritance that He will never deprive me of. God bestowed upon us the gift of family, and as each of our family members seeks His guidance, He will offer them assistance. Jesus himself said this in *Matt. 18:19-20, "Again I say to you, if two of you agree on earth about anything they ask, it will be done for them by my Father in heaven. For where two or three are gathered in my name, there am I among them."*

Would you like to join me in looking into the distance for a glimpse of our daughter's/mother's return? After all, if the God of the Bible is the God of restoration, who are we to tell God he breaks his promises? So look up, look out, and look ahead. Hebrews 11:1 reminds us to look toward what we hope for. *Heb. 11:1, "Now faith is the assurance of things hoped for, the conviction of things not seen."*

Journal

1. Think of a time when you did not have an expectant mindset.
2. Are you still embracing expectancy?
3. What is holding you back from having an expectant heart?
4. Do you trust the process of healing, not your pain?
5. As you restore yourself to the love of God, your expectant heart will prepare you for the days that haven't come yet.
6. A prayer of salvation and a pleading of God to solve what seems unsolvable:

   Jesus, I humbly approach you with my shattered relationships and my complete being. I am grateful for your sacrifice on the cross, which was made specifically for me. I dedicate my life to you wholeheartedly. Holy Spirit please come near me, fall on me and live within me all the days of my life.

   Heavenly Father, I express my gratitude for granting Jesus complete authority over my life. Jesus, I affirm that through the strength of your name, all obstacles restraining complete healing in my mother's life, my daughter's life, and my own life will be overcome for your glory. May every chain be broken against any adversary standing in the way of restoration.

   Thank you, Jesus, for all that you have already accomplished. I will trust you even in my moments of pain. I have hope for a complete restoration of the abundant and delightful inheritance that you, God, had planned for me long before you, God, formed the heavens and the earth.

Thank you Holy Spirit for being near me, and you are welcome to transform me by your wisdom in every area of my life.

Amen.

At Estrangement, Moms & Daughters on www.skool.com, women are warmly invited to create new friendships with women who understand the anguish and hope of growing through the grief and rebuilding of estrangement. We may be without our mother/daughters but we do not have to be alone. Join our warm community that will encourage you to love yourself and to overcome ruminating patterns holding you back. Come celebrate one another where we hold each other as highly valued. It is possible to give hope, share hope, and look far into the horizon for resolution with self and others.

Bibliography

Everett L. Worthington Jr PhD 1, Charlotte VanOyen Witvliet PhD 2, Andrea J. Lerner BS 1, Michael Scherer MS 1. "Forgiveness in Health Research and Medical Practice." Explore Volume 1, issue 3, may 2005, pages 169-176. Accessed Feb. 16, 2024, https://www.sciencedirect.com/science/article/abs/pii/S155083 0705001540

Gilbert, Alphonso Dr. (Men of Valor Prison Ministries), interviews by Jodi Cunningham, January 2024. Tenn.

Graham, Ruth, Forgiving My Father, Forgiving Myself: An Invitation to the Miricle of Forgiveness: Grand Rapids, MI: Baker Books 2019.

Grief.com. "Because Love Never Dies." Accessed January 19, 2024. https://grief.com/the-five-stages-of-grief/

Hogan, Shelly Dr. (Owner of e5lifestrategies), interviewed by Jodi Cunningham, December 2023. Zoom, Phoenix AZ. https://www.e5lifestrategies.com

Keller, Tim. Gospel in Life, Mary's son. Episode 983. Podcast audio. November 15, 2023. Accessed Feb. 16, 2024, https://podcast.gospelinlife.com/e/mary-s-son-1700058255/

Lisita, Ellie. Gottman.com. "The Four Horsemen: Criticism, Contempt, Defensiveness, and Stonewalling." Accessed January 19, 2024. https://grief.com/the-five-stages-of-grief/

Miesner, Bob Dr. (lead partner/owner of Love Married Life), interviewed by Jodi Cunningham, January, 2024. Zoom, Phoenix Az. https://www.lovemarriedlife.com/

NPR.org. " Take the Ace Quiz—And Learn What it Does and Doesn't Mean." March 2, 2015. Accessed Feb. 16, 2024, https://www.npr.org/sections/health-shots/2015/03/02/387007941/take-the-ace-quiz-and-learn-what-it-does-and-doesnt-mean

Warren, Cortney Dr. Wed, Jan 3, 2024. "Harvard psychologist: If you say 'yes' to any of these 9 questions, you're 'more emotionally secure than most." CNBC MAKE It. Accessed Jan. 28, 2024. https://www.cnbc.com/2024/01/03/harvard-psychologist-if-you-answer-yes-to-any-of-these-questions-youre-more-emotionally-secure-than-most-people.html

Wiesenthal, Simon, The Sunflower: Paris: Manufactured in the United States, Schocken Books 1976.

YouTube. 2015. "Plato's Allegory of the Cave." Accessed Feb. 16, 2024. www.youtube.com/watch?v=1RWOpQXTltA

About the Author

Jodi LaRae Cunningham is a mother of two adult children. She owns LaRae Faith Ballroom Fashions. She is an author strategist at Authors on Mission. She has a master's degree in divinity. She is a licensed chaplain with Intl Fellowship of Chaplains. She attends ChurchLV in Henderson, NV. She assists 65-plus children in Mityana, Uganda who live within the orphanage called Artists Against Hunger. There she has helped to provide the girls a safe home and the boys a farm home. The boys and girls in Mityana farm a 10-acre field, named the Isaiah Faith Fields in honor of her children. It is her hope that all who read this will know their value and will live a life abundantly full of good moments, solid friendships, and a hope for today and the future.

Made in the USA
Las Vegas, NV
12 February 2025

18061429R00083